S0-AJE-919

For Reinhard Kuhn,
very cordially.

R. Selvich

UNIVERSITY OF NORTH CAROLINA
STUDIES IN THE ROMANCE LANGUAGES AND LITERATURES
Number 83

ROUSSEAU AND HIS READER:
THE RHETORICAL SITUATION OF THE MAJOR WORKS

ROUSSEAU AND HIS READER: THE RHETORICAL SITUATION OF THE MAJOR WORKS

BY

ROBERT J. ELLRICH

CHAPEL HILL

THE UNIVERSITY OF NORTH CAROLINA PRESS

PRINTED IN SPAIN

DEPÓSITO LEGAL: V. 3.132 - 1969

ARTES GRÁFICAS SOLER, S. A. - JÁVEA, 30 - VALENCIA (8) - 1969

TABLE OF CONTENTS

FOREWORD

The idea for this study first took form during a year of reduced teaching responsibilities made possible by a grant from the Council of the Humanities of Princeton University, to which I am happy to express my gratitude. A summer grant from the University of Washington provided me with additional free time to pursue the topic, and for this too I am most grateful.

It is a pleasure, as well, to acknowledge the aid given me by friends and colleagues, among whom I will single out for especial thanks Karl D. Uitti, whose suggestions and encouragement were of invaluable assistance, and Richard L. Frautschi, whose remarkably careful reading of the manuscript permitted me to smooth many rough edges.

Finally, I extend sincere and cordial recognition to the students who have participated in my seminars on Rousseau at Princeton University and the University of Washington. The dialogue that we have maintained has been perhaps the most important factor in helping me think through the various problems involved in the study. I am particularly indebted to Robert Von Dassow for his insights into the rhetorical situation of the *Rêveries du promeneur solitaire*.

* * *

I have used for reference, wherever possible, the Gallimard *Œuvres complètes* of Rousseau. Unfortunately, as of this writing only the first three volumes have appeared. For works not yet published by Gallimard, I have gone to the recognized critical edition, or, in cases where no such authoritative text exists, to the original edition. For the *Emile,* however, from which I have had to quote copiously, I decided to use the Garnier edition, the only good one widely available.

R. J. E.

Seattle, Washington
August, 1968

"[...] nothing the writer does can be finally understood in isolation from his effort to make it all accessible to someone else — his peers, himself as imagined reader, his audience." (Wayne Booth, *The Rhetoric of Fiction*.)

INTRODUCTION

My purpose in this study is to analyze Rousseau's relationship to his reader in the major works from the *Discours sur les sciences et les arts* to the *Rêveries du promeneur solitaire*. I have chosen the major works alone largely for reasons of economy, since to deal with the entire corpus of writings would add an enormous burden of material without furnishing a commensurate gain in understanding. Moreover, while dealing principally with a particular aspect of Rousseau's work, I do not wish to address myself merely to Rousseau specialists, but hope to reach as well the fairly broad audience of readers possessing a direct acquaintance with some of the major works and at least an indirect knowledge of the rest. In this way I may be able to accomplish a secondary aim: to stimulate further thought and discussion on the general subject of the writer-reader relationship in literature.

Because of the indecisiveness of our current state of knowledge in matters pertaining to language and communication, any inquiry into the relationship between writer and reader runs the risk of ending up richer in hypotheses than in certainties. The principles and models employed thus far seem at best incomplete, at worst irrelevant, and the critics from Aristotle on who have ventured to explore this crucial area of literary analysis, courageous and perceptive though they may have been, resemble the early cartographers, who mixed empirical evidence with hearsay and drew their maps without benefit of sure principles of geodesy. Still, it is tempting to believe that the recent explosion of interest in rhetoric —both in its traditional definitions and manifestations and in its more modern sense of all those aspects of a literary work having to do with the relationship between writer and reader— may eventually result in a firmer grasp of its nature and operations. (Since a persistent problem in recent studies has been the lack of standard vocabulary, I shall explain from the beginning that I use the term *rhetorical situation*, which appears in the sub-title and will recur in the text, to designate the relationship in a given work between the writer and the reader as this relationship is embodied in the form.)

Although I shall save the bulk of theoretical statement for those places where it can be made in connection with an appropriate text, a few preliminary remarks concerning my working models and hypotheses are in order. They are basically those of the structural linguists and semiologists (such as Roman Jakobson) and of the recent students of rhetoric (especially Wayne Booth). I have, however, avoided as much as possible the specialized terminology of these scholars since the layman's language is adequate to my purposes and allows, again, for a wider audience. My initial principle is simple and familiar: All use of speech implies convention and therefore at least duality of minds. The problem of communication through language may in this light be seen as the search for the means supplied by the conventions (or code) to transmit a message from one mind to another. (This definition is as applicable to "literary" communication as it is to "non-literary.") Deceptively clear in its broadest formulation, the statement begs endless questions as soon as we begin to examine its terms and to introduce variables. Is the code exactly the same for transmitter and receiver? Indeed, can it ever be? It hardly seems likely, since in the strict sense no two people have ever acquired exactly the same code. Consequently, the correspondence between the writer's understanding of his writing (I do not, of course, mean merely a conscious or reflective understanding) and the reader's understanding of it will be at best approximate. Another variable is the mental, emotional, and cultural constitution of the being who uses the code to transmit a message, and of the being who decodes it. To what extent are they capable of understanding each other? To what extent will they be willing to cooperate in dealing with the inevitable problems in communication? To what extent will anticipated or actual reaction ("feedback") from the receiver affect the framing of the message? Perhaps more important than any of these variables, there is the as yet unresolved question of the very nature of language, and therefore of communication through language. What do the agreed-upon symbols *stand for?* Is it conceivable that they correspond to something objectively identifiable? Perhaps not. But even if so, is it conceivable that a given message can recreate in another mind whatever it is supposed in the first place to represent in the mind of the sender? All of these questions are in the last analysis as relevant to literary studies as they are linguistics.

We run into only slightly lesser problems with the notion itself of "reader." Precisely who or what is the reader? There is, of course, the actual reader, a specific person who decodes —or tries to decode— the written message, and who differs from a listener only in that he cannot influence the flow of discourse with his interventions. The identity of this reader may, to be sure, be known to the writer, and this knowledge will become a factor in the framing of the message. (To appreciate Rousseau's own awareness of and sensitivity to the reader in this sense, one need only read his account of the differing replies he wrote in defense of his First Discourse, the one directed to King Stanislas of Poland and the other to a gentleman in Nancy for whom he had no respect.) [1] Then too, if the specific identity of the real reader is unknown to the writer at the time of writing, a response after the fact will provide the "feedback" that in turn influences the framing of later messages. This particular factor, primarily psychological and social in nature, will play a crucial role in the evolution of the rhetorical situation of Rousseau's works.

In addition to the individual reader, there is an aggregate of readers —a public— with whose expectations, conventions, and habitual reactions the writer is familiar. Although any or many of the individual readers making up this aggregate may never become actual readers of the work, by their very existence they exert an influence upon the writer. In this regard, the notions of "reader" and of "rhetorical situation" take on historical and sociological dimensions the nature of which the critic must

---

[1] *Œuvres complètes,* Paris (Gallimard), 1959-, vol. I, pp. 365-366. Unless otherwise specified, all references involving Rousseau's writings are to this edition, abbreviated henceforth to *O. C.*

understand and the pressure of which he must take into account. Now, the process of artistic creation through which the writer selects his formal representations (including the minutest points of style) is basically dialogic: the awareness of and concern for other minds translates itself into auto-criticism, which in turn directs esthetic choice. Through a gradual formation analogous to that of conscience in the moral domain, there develops in every writer a faculty of judgement —called "taste" in the 18th century— permitting him to determine the appropriate means for achieving particular effects in verbal communication. [2] In brief, he learns to know, respect, and respond to the limitations, the expectancies, and in general the reactive possibilities of the public; to whose reactive possibilities he may, of course, add through a process of education.

No writer, however, is ever confronted with a homogeneous group of readers. In Rousseau's time, the public was fragmented not only ideologically but in terms of literary expectancies as well. We will see that he keeps in mind therefore various sub-groupings defined by nationality, moral notions, religion, sex, profession, rank, etc., and at the same time sub-groupings of, for example, more or less normative readers of neo-classical formation and somewhat more flexible, and frequently younger, readers sympathetic to the innovations in form and subject matter sweeping through mid-century France. (Voltaire's scandalized reaction to the "âcre baiser" implanted by Julie on Saint-Preux's lips is characteristic of the more conservative reader.) A highly conscious writer to begin with, Rousseau was endowed with an extraordinary sense of historical moment and an intuitive under-standing of sociological distinctions. Moreover, his frequent assertions to the contrary notwithstanding, he was vastly interested

---

2 Seen in this light, all aspects of form are a function of the rhetorical situation. The significant distinction among them resides in the degree of overtness of the relationship between writer and reader. Traditional discussions of rhetoric, originating in considerations of the art of persuasion, took as their object of study only these conscious, and for the most part voluntary, aspects of expression. No discussion of the relation of technique to effect or of form to meaning can, however, ignore the broader problems (and search for solutions) that lie behind every *attempt* the writer makes to transmit a specific message to a reader. There is, in addition, some question as to whether persuasion is not an element of all communication.

in obtaining as wide an audience as possible — if only to castigate certain segments of it. His conception of his public will therefore be highly conscious, sophisticated, and varied.

Whom he is addressing will be one of Rousseau's persistent concerns. Throughout the great period of his "public doctrine" (1750-1762), he writes as a prophet aware of his mission, bringing a vision of truth to the unredeemed reader. He proudly identifies himself to the reader by signing his works, a gesture considered unusual at the time, at least on the part of an author of fiction or of possibly controversial works. During the apologetic period (1762-1776) he becomes, as we shall see, increasingly obsessed with establishing and maintaining lines of communication with a reader. And at the end of his life, at the beginning of the *Rêveries,* one of his first questions still is to whom he shall address himself, now that he is "cut off from all men."

The depth of Rousseau's attachment to his works in itself reflects the urgency of his sense of relationship to his reader. Perhaps more than any previous French writer he was a devoted father to his books. He tended to produce multiple copies of them (four of *La Nouvelle Héloïse!*), partly no doubt in order to relive the initial pleasure of creation, but partly to insure their safe arrival in a reader's hands. He continued, moreover, to defend his spiritual offspring as long as he felt that there remained a chance of making them understood to the public. Hence in nearly all his works, up to and including the *Dialogues,* the presence of footnotes serving to clarify or develop certain points, to explain his method, to forestall anticipated objections, or to reply to criticism made after the first edition of the work. In nearly all cases, the notes are inspired by the writer's awareness of his reader and of the problems involved in his relationship with his reader (who can so easily misunderstand). In the last analysis, Rousseau's obsession with placing a manuscript of the *Dialogues* in reliable custody to preserve it for posterity, culminating in the famous attempt to deposit a copy of it on the High Altar of Notre Dame (i.e., under God's protection) is merely an extreme manifestation of a persistent concern with communication.

Rousseau's hyperawareness of the relationship with his reader is a literary manifestation of his obsession with the distinction between Self and Other, and with the concomitant problems of identity, self-definition, and conflict of minds and wills. His essential problem in conceiving of and dealing with his reader may be stated quite simply: a deep longing for perfect union between himself and his reader finds itself countered by the painful recognition, and eventual anticipation, of the reader's failure to enter into this perfect union. The conflict that thus arises, explored in its psychological dimensions, its various formal manifestations, and its evolution over a period of nearly three decades, will be the main subject of my study.

Rousseau suffered from what might be described as "anguish of communication." In an important passage in the Third Book of the *Confessions* (too lengthy to reproduce here in its entirety), Rousseau reflects upon this feeling and upon its consequences. [3] What he says is highly revealing both by direct statement and by implication. Concerning his embarrassment in conversation, he claims not to be able to understand how one dares speak in company: "car à chaque mot il faudroit passer en revue tous les gens qui sont là: il faudroit connoitre tous leurs caractéres, savoir leurs histoires pour être sur de ne rien dire qui puisse offenser quelqu'un." Added to the fear of offending (and probably related to it), there is the intolerable feeling of constraint in a situation that, in Rousseau's mind, demands speech regardless of the immediate inclination. Having established these points, Rousseau goes on to observe: "Le parti que j'ai pris d'écrire et de me cacher est précisément celui qui me convenoit. Moi présent on n'auroit jamais su ce que je valois, on ne l'auroit pas soupçonné même." I submit that the grammatical parallel between *me cacher* and *écrire* tells us more than Rousseau would perhaps intentionally have us know. Writing has an advantage over speech, in that it allows us to hide preliminary stages of thought, to eliminate inconsistencies, hesitations, etc., and to appear, in brief, in a better light than we might in an oral confrontation. In this regard, a metaphor introduced by Rousseau in the same passage to describe how his ideas, at first confused and chaotic, slowly take form in his head during the process of composition, reveals the self-protective motive in Rousseau's preference for the written word over the spoken:

---

[3] *O. C.*, I, pp. 113-116.

N'avez-vous point vu quelquefois l'Opera en Italie? Dans les changemens de scène il règne sur ces grands théatres un desordre desagréable, et qui dure assez longtems: toutes les décorations sont entre mêlées; on voit de toutes parts un tiraillement qui fait peine; on croit que tout va renverser. Cependant peu à peu tout s'arrange, rien ne manque, et l'on est tout surpris de voir succéder à ce long tumulte un spectacle ravissant. Cette manoeuvre est à peu près celle qui se fait dans mon cerveau quand je veux écrire.

As a writer, Rousseau may himself be aware of the "unpleasant disorder" in his mind, but he can draw the curtain between it and his reader, to whom he presents only the "ravishing spectacle."

When the fear of —the obsession with— response from another reaches such proportions, we should expect that even within the protected domain of the written word there would appear degrees of preference. Not surprisingly, Rousseau states (in the passage under consideration) his intense dislike for correspondence. The existence of a specific, known reader is menacing, and the letter becomes a "long et confus verbiage." One might postulate a descending order of preference in verbal communication: talking to oneself (as Rousseau will understand himself to be doing in his *Rêveries*); writing highly controlled discourse with no specific reader in mind; writing to a specific reader; talking to friends (as in certain privileged moments with Mme de Warens and Mme d'Houdetot); talking to strangers or enemies. Rousseau states that he found an inhibiting virtue in the very sight of writing implements, and claims to use language freely only during his meditative walks or while lying awake at night. Pen, paper, and writing-desk are doubtless unsettling reminders that his words will cease to be his sole property, and will be at the mercy of a reader.

Still, we are primarily interested here in the preference for writing over speech, or reader over interlocutor. In this regard, we may derive oblique elucidation from a study of the rhetorical situation built into *La Nouvelle Héloïse*. Just as Rousseau's own relationship to his reader is determined by his notion of relationship between self and other, so the epistolary relationship (a writer-reader relationship) among the characters of his novel will be shaped by this same notion. We may expect, then, to see in the rhetorical situation found in the letters significant parallels with the rhetorical situation in Rousseau's "reader-directed" writings. Indeed, the nature and dynamics of the epistolary relationships may reveal in *clearer* light some of the deeper motivations and mechanisms that in Rousseau's own relationship to his reader are slightly veiled by defensiveness and self-consciousness.

One fact stands out: the letters are frequently addressed to a person who is either directly available for verbal communication or who has been removed by the author simply to provide the occasion for letter-writing. The first three letters, for example, are addressed by Saint-Preux to Julie, yet they are members of the same household and can meet without constraint. Nonetheless, when Saint-Preux has a message of importance to transmit (when he reveals his love to her), he writes. (The opening sentence of the novel sets the stage for this peculiar distancing: "Il faut vous fuir, mademoiselle.") Another example, perhaps more striking, is to be found in Part I, Letter 14, where Saint-Preux, waiting for Julie to arrive in her bed-chamber (where he is hidden), writes to her of his feelings instead of waiting to *tell* her of them. He goes so far as to describe her own arrival as it takes place (this in a letter addressed to her!): "C'est elle! je l'entrevois, je l'ai vûe, j'entends fermer la porte." [4] In the following letter, he describes to her his feelings during the "nuit inconcevable" they have just spent together; and it is just as well, for to judge by his own description the lovers were entirely mute throughout the experience itself. He gives no account of any verbal exchange, listing instead: "étroite union des âmes [...] abbatement si doux [...] sommeil enchanteur [...] réveil plus doux encore [...] soupirs entrecoupés [...] baisers [...] gémissemens." The characters of the novel always seem oddly constrained verbally in one another's presence (this constraint gives way once to triumph and

---

[4] These distancing procedures are not to be explained merely by reference to the needs and conventions of the epistolary form. Rousseau could easily have found other ways of presenting the material. That he should not have chosen to avoid such an obvious implausibility would seem in itself to suggest a motive for presenting the material thus and not otherwise.

delight in the magical, *non-verbal* communication of feeling during the "matinée à l'anglaise"), but in writing they are remarkably open and communicative. Clearly, the act of communication through writing rather than through speech has a special significance for Rousseau. He wrote eloquent letters that he never sent (for example to the "homme au beurre"); he devised a new system of musical notation; he was a capyist by profession, and in fact loved to recopy his own works.

As we have seen, writing allows for the protection of a narcissistic image of oneself, and in general serves to protect the writer against a hostile response. (Rousseau's wry comment that he would carry on a lovely conversation by mail, "comme on dit que les Espagnols jouent aux échecs," [5] reveals through the image how hostile an activity he conceived conversation to be.) If writing has this advantage over speech, it is because the writer is alone, and freer to fantasize than the speaker. The control that is the essence of fantasy permits not only the protection of a narcissistic self-image, but the illusions of autonomy, power, and gratification of desire. In the letter already quoted, Saint-Preux pauses in the heat of his amorous fantasies (woven about Julie's expected arrival) to remark: "Quel bonheur d'avoir trouvé de l'encre et du papier! J'exprime ce que je sens pour en tempérer l'excès, je donne le change à mes transports en les décrivant." Writing appears as an auto-erotic act (the common 18th-century euphemism for masturbation being "donner le change à la nature"). [6] It thus provides a means of either anticipating or reenacting *in fantasy* the actual contact, whether verbal or physical. In speaking of his early masturbatory experiences, Rousseau points out the advantage of fantasy precisely in terms of control: "Ce vice que la honte et la timidité trouvent si commode, a de plus un grand attrait pour les imaginations vives; c'est de disposer pour ainsi dire à leur gré de tout le sexe, et de faire servir à leurs plaisirs la beauté qui les tente sans avoir besoin d'obtenir son aveu." [7] The analogy, invited

---

[5] *O. C.* I, p. 113.

[6] The same need to "exprimer l'excès" at a distance from the object of the fantasy can be seen in Rousseau's account of his frequent walks from the Hermitage to Eaubonne to see Mme d'Houdetot (*O. C.* I, p. 445).

[7] *O. C.* I, p. 109.

by Rousseau's own reference to the "imaginations vives," rings true in terms of the advantage of writing over speaking (in direct confrontation). Needless to say, the writer too can be "seduced" into conceiving for himself a reader who feeds back only what is convenient and agreeable, who understands without effort exactly what the writer wishes him to understand, and who provides, so to speak, the fulfillment of the writer's every desire.

In dealing with Rousseau, one must confront a paradox of change wedded to changelessness. His essential "doctrine," based on the principles expressed in the First Discourse, remains invariable throughout his writings. Yet critics have pointed time and again to apparent contradictions in the elaboration and the ramifications of the doctrine. His character and vision, as Jean Starobinski has demonstrated,[8] were originally shaped and later governed by certain motives and conceptions to which he clung unremittingly. And yet he was prone to adopt various identities (including pseudonyms), given to sudden, extreme shifts in mood, and possessed of contradictory moral qualities. As one might expect, the rhetorical situation of his works reflects these divergencies. Rousseau tries out different kinds of relationship to his reader, with varying postures and tones, and frequently operates with diverse notions of his reader within a single work. Still more important a trait for our purposes, however, is his vacillation between admiration for the ideal as alone worthy of human regard and condemnation of the same ideal as pernicious illusion. An understanding of the evolution of the rhetorical situation of his works depends upon the recognition of this antinomy. As his growing awareness of partial or total failure in communication with a real reader (with whom perfect communication is impossible) competes with his persistent desire for perfect communication with an ideal reader (alone capable of such communication),[9] Rousseau will first attempt various solu-

---

[8] *Jean-Jacques Rousseau. La Transparence et l'obstacle,* Paris (Plon), 1958. My own understanding of Rousseau owes much to Professor Starobinski's work, and I am happy to acknowledge the debt.

[9] It is important to keep in mind that for the writer engaged in writing, the reader is an internalized figure. He is the writer's fantasy, and this is true whether the writer is composing a poem, a novel, or a scientific paper. There enters into the consideration, however, a crucially important variable

tions and evasions, during the period of public doctrine. Then, no longer able to avoid the increasing conflictual tension, he will pass through two major crises of rhetorical orientation. The first, occasioned by a questioning of his role as purveyor of truth, will occur in the early to middle 1760's, with the *Emile* as the critical event and the great letters (to Malesherbes, to Christophe de Beaumont, and the *Lettres écrites de la montagne*) as the pivots by which he turns towards personal revelation and self-justification. During the apologetic period, Rousseau will be largely concerned with appropriating the reader, turning the reader into another self, and thus insuring perfect communication. The second crisis, poignant and mysterious, will be the abandonment, during the summer of 1776, of both his chimerical pursuit of perfect union with an ideal reader and of his by now maniacal obsession with self-justification. The product of this second crisis will be the ember-fires of the *Rêveries du promeneur solitaire,* the rhetorical situation of which differs from that of the earlier works in that the writer now recognizes and accepts the autonomy of the reader.

Inevitably, the nature of the problems I shall be dealing with in this book, along with the avenues of exploration and the conclusions to which they lead, cannot at this point be entirely clear to my own reader. If such were the case, there would be little point in his reading on. This is, however, sufficiently brief a

---

in the form of the writer's particular psychological set: To what extent does he wish, or is he able, to hold in mind a notion of the reader that corresponds to an objectively existent reader? In a sense, every writer creates the reader he wants, shaping him in advance according to his fantasy, and this process is perhaps what all writing and reading are about. But the process is beset with problems, tensions, and (ultimately) limitations, which the critic must take into account, discerning the problems relevant to a particular writer or work and analyzing the means by which the writer has actualized his fantasy. I have found in my study of Rousseau that one issue, although not of exclusive importance, is of highest relevance: the writer's obsession with an ideal reader. The absolute nature of his fantasy reader —whom he would wish to be virtually a mind-reader— will lead Rousseau to lose, in effect, his sense of the identity and capacities of a real reader or group of readers, and thus his ability, as a writer, to narrow the gap between the real reader and the fantasy. In other terms, Rousseau will take too much for granted, and as a result will encounter unexpected trouble in "shaping" the reader for a proper understanding of his message.

study to permit of a cumulative understanding of its subject, and I would only echo here Rousseau's own frequent exhortation to his reader to have patience: "Je ne peux pas tout dire à la fois."

CHAPTER I

THE EASY SOLUTIONS

During the period of his public doctrine (1750-1762), Rousseau entertains with his reader the kind of relationship typical of one who has passed through a conversion experience. The sudden illumination on the road to Vincennes endowed him with the unshakeable conviction that he *knew* the truth of man's nature, the causes of his corruption, and the path back to innocence. In the *Discours sur les sciences et les arts* he proclaims the existence of a cultural disorder, exhorting mankind to recognize and remedy it. In the *Discours sur l'inégalité* he turns his efforts to providing an historical and functional analysis of the disorder. Then, having described in full the nature and history of man's decline, he presents to the world his vision of the redeemed society and of the means of redemption, producing in a five-year period of intense creativity the *Lettre à d'Alembert, La Nouvelle Héloïse, Du Contrat social,* and the *Emile.* From the First Discourse to the *Emile,* his relationship to his reader reflects a deep feeling of confidence in his rôle as messiah, as purveyor of truth. Analysis of the individual works will demonstrate how easy a task it seemed to gain adherence to a truth that the writer considered self-evident.

Yet all is not well. From the start there creeps in an uneasiness that Rousseau will disregard until, in the writing and defense of the *Emile,* he can no longer manage to do so. In 1762, he will write to Malesherbes in reference to his illumination:

> Oh Monsieur si j'avois jamais pû ecrire le quart de
> ce que j'ai vû et senti sous cet arbre, avec quelle clarté
> j'aurois fait voir toutes les contradictions du systeme so-
> cial, avec quelle force j'aurois exposé tous les abus de nos
> institutions, avec quelle simplicité j'aurois demontré que
> l'homme est bon naturellement et que c'est par ces institu-
> tions seules que les hommes deviennent méchans. Tout
> ce que j'ai pu retenir de ces foules de grandes vérités
> qui dans un quart d'heure m'illuminerent sous cet arbre,
> a eté bien foiblement epars dans les trois principaux de
> mes ecrits [. . . .] [1]

Here the writer recognizes his relative failure in communicating
his vision, although he chooses to see it as an internal failure
due to the intervention of the demon Time: between the writer's
vision and his external representation of it through the mediation
of language there is a fatal moment during which the vision fades.
Although in part a rationalization, this explanation nonetheless
constitutes an implicit recognition of failure in perfect communication of the truth Rousseau himself had seen. This recognition will, however, be held below the surface during the twelve-
year period under study in this chapter. Rousseau seems to accept
during this period the principle of Socratic optimism: it is possible to show men the truth, which they will then unfailingly
adopt. Any questioning of this principle, any uneasiness in the
role of messiah will come out only by indirection, as we shall see
in the use of certain defensive strategies. As long as Rousseau
adheres to the notion of himself as a messiah with the unfailing
ability to convince the world of his truth, he will create for
himself a reader-figure just as convinceable and malleable as
Socrates' own interlocutors.

❖ ❖ ❖

DISCOURS SUR LES SCIENCES ET LES ARTS (1750)

No work by Rousseau, with the possible exception of the
Emile (a pivotal work, as we shall see), displays greater complexity

---

[1] *O. C.* I, pp. 1135-6.

and variety in its rhetorical situation than the First Discourse. In it Rousseau not only lays the foundation for all of his future doctrine but provides as well an initial glimpse of all of the important aspects and modes of his relationship with his reader.

Already in his prefatory address to the members of the Académie de Dijon, who had proposed the topic of the discourse, Rousseau provides the first hint of his sense of independence as a writer. He refers to himself with arrogant modesty as one who speaks to them in the role of "un honnête homme qui ne sait rien, et qui ne s'en estime pas moins," [2] an embryonic statement of his later confidence in his own ability to uncover the truth without recourse to conventional wisdom or traditional knowledge. A still clearer expression of this sense of independence and self-reliance appears shortly thereafter: "après avoir soutenu, selon ma lumière naturelle, le parti de la vérité; quel que soit mon succès, il est un Prix qui ne peut me manquer: Je le trouverai dans le fond de mon cœur." The assertion points towards Rousseau's conception of himself as his *own* reader and judge. He is in fact serving notice on the Academicians supposedly judging his work that they are not his reader; their prize is a mere accessory. Characteristic of Rousseau's attitude as a writer, this declaration of independence is doubtless based partly on a fear of rejection or miscomprehension, partly on a deep longing for complete self-sufficiency that will lead finally to a rhetorical solipsism of sorts.

Whatever his motivations may be, Rousseau clearly anticipates his reader's disapproval: "Je prévois qu'on me pardonnera difficilement le parti que j'ai osé prendre. Heurtant de front tout ce qui fait aujourd'hui l'admiration des hommes, je ne puis m'attendre qu'à un blâme universel." [3] He is concerned then —if by disclaimer— not only with the judgment of the Académie; he anticipates the hostility of all readers ("blâme *universel*"). Destined to become an obsession later in Rousseau's career, this expectation occurs in the First Discourse only as a preliminary (although significant) remark, and controls hardly at all the presentation of the material. It is related, however, to what I

---

[2] *O. C.* III, p. 5.
[3] Ibid., p. 3.

would call Rousseau's fundamental posture in the work, his presentation of himself to the reader as the virtuous outsider. Rousseau's choice of epigraph for his discourse (from Ovid's *Tristia*) is revealing: "Barbarus hic ego sum quia non intelligor illis." Speaking the unknown language of nature and morality, he expects to be misunderstood and to be considered an outsider.

The initial kernel of the First Discourse, the passage known as the "prosopopée de Fabricius," supposedly composed by Rousseau during the white heat of his "conversion experience" on the road to Vincennes, gives the model of the rhetorical situation of the entire work. Rousseau imagines Fabricius (the republican Roman statesman renowned for his austere virtue) returning to Rome, long after his own death and after Rome's transition from republic to empire. He harangues his fellow countrymen —now strangers to him— on their decline and exhorts them to adopt once more the virtuous simplicity of their forebears. Now, we know that Rousseau admired above all men the eminent figures of the Roman Republic, and that he was wont during his childhood even to fancy himself as one or another of them. Fabricius would thus appear as a kind of *alter ego* to Jean-Jacques Rousseau. Jean-Jacques himself was fond of reminding the French that he was the citizen of a republic. In addition, he too, like Fabricius, had stepped out of past time (or so he liked to think), the time of the Arcadian world of goodness, simplicity, and virtue in which he tells us he lived as a child, and which he was always to consider his true mother country. Thus, he appears morally, temporally, and geographically a stranger, and, again like Fabricius, addresses a civilization by which, through being an outsider, he is uncorrupted. This is the conception of himself in relation to his audience that directs and shapes the rhetoric of his discourse. Much of the work resounds with the tribunal eloquence that Rousseau had learned from Cicero and Plutarch: he harangues, he admonishes, he castigates, he exhorts, using all the standard rhetorical figures appropriate to the forensic tradition. As his anticipation of rejection is still relatively undeveloped, his hope for influencing, perhaps even reshaping, the corrupt civilization is proportionately strong. This point is of considerable importance, for Rousseau's belief in his role as messiah and his ultimate disappointment in that role will prove to be one of the major factors in the evolution of his sense of relationship with the reader, and hence of his situation as a writer attempting to bridge the gap between minds.

The corrupt civilization that Rousseau addresses in the First Discourse is not merely 18th-century French urban culture. Rousseau had a marked tendency to attempt to escape from the ordinary restrictions of time, either ignoring temporal flow by living in an absolute present or ignoring the present to live in the past, the future, or even in a hypothetical time bearing no relationship to past, present, or future. In the First Discourse, he ressuscitates past time, as easily as he does Fabricius, and addresses mankind past and present with equal immediacy. Ancient peoples, as if gathered before him, are praised for their virtues and blamed for their vices. Modern philosophers are addressed with scorn and irony. Rousseau speaks from his tribunal to the living and the dead. One can see this synchronic conception of his audience in the synchronically inclusive use of the first-person plural that will recur in Rousseau's later writings: "Avant que l'Art eut façonné nos manières et appris à nos passions à parler un langage apprêté, nos moeurs étoient rustiques, mais naturelles"; "Voilà comment le luxe, la dissolution et l'esclavage ont été de tout tems le châtiment des efforts orgueilleux que nous avons faits pour sortir de l'heureuse ignorance." [4]

This breakdown of barriers of time (and of space, as the prevalent use of apostrophe indicates) is symptomatic of Rousseau's deep-rooted tendency to manipulate his conception of the reader in ways that seem startling in the works of a "philosophical" writer. There are processes at work here that suggest the artist's recreation of reality rather than the descriptive and analytic enterprise of the thinker, a fact that should not surprise us now that we recognize the essentially artistic, imaginative nature of Rousseau's genius. These same processes, however, will give rise to problems of communication with the real reader, because of Rousseau's eventual replacement of the real reader (with whom he is, after all, attempting to establish communication) by an ideal reader of his own creation. The intense desire to communicate

----

[4] Ibid., pp. 8, 15.

perfectly, as if magically, with his reader will lead ironically to a breakdown in communication.

The fantasy of perfect communication, destroying barriers of time, space, and the inevitable opacity of human beings, betokens a desire for solidarity that might seem to contradict Rousseau's declarations of independence and his adoption of the posture of the outsider. The fact is, however, that here as elsewhere in Rousseau there exists a precarious equilibrium between desire for independence and counterdesire for perfect communion. (Hence for example, the satisfaction he derives from the idea of a social contract permitting each individual to give himself completely to the collectivity without losing his freedom.)

✻   ✻   ✻

The features discussed so far represent, in germinal form, the characteristic elements and tendencies to be found in Rousseau's rhetorical situation. Through the following twelve years, no crucial changes will occur. The moment of crisis, when the tensions inherent in the situation will oblige Rousseau to feel his way towards a new rhetorical orientation, will come, as mentioned, with the writing, publication, and defense of the *Emile*. The great public works of the period 1750-1762 follow, by and large, the patterns established in the First Discourse. Each of the works from this period, however, will show Rousseau trying out his relationship with both the real and the ideal reader in different ways, with varying points of emphasis, gradations of concern, and distinctions in emotional coloration.

✻   ✻   ✻

DISCOURS SUR L'ORIGINE ET LES FONDEMENTS DE L'INÉGALITÉ
    PARMI LES HOMMES (1755)

Rousseau had anticipated that his *Discours sur les sciences et les arts* would elicit criticism, but even he could hardly have known in advance just how painful society would find his probing into its cultural decay. According to the Abbé de La Porte, writing two years after the event, the publication of the discourse gave rise to a literary quarrel in which all of France seemingly took part. [5] Whatever may have been the relative percentage of admirers to detractors, Rousseau reacted with characteristic defensiveness towards the latter and quickly moved to the counterattack. His own comments concerning his reader (this time the actual reading public) reveal his concern with public miscomprehension and hostility. Already in the preface to *Narcisse* (1752) [6] this note is struck, although without the tone of bitterness and discouragement that will so often prevail later on: "Je conseille donc à ceux qui sont si ardens à chercher des reproches à me faire, de vouloir mieux étudier mes principes et mieux observer ma conduite, avant que de m'y taxer de contradiction et d'inconséquence." [7] The notation is discreet in this early instance. It will become more insistent as Rousseau experiences further difficulties.

In composing his *Discours sur l'inégalité* Rousseau seems, however, less concerned with defending his doctrine against attack than with giving it an historical foundation and presenting it in what was meant to be a thoroughly comprehensible and irrefutable fashion. His basic posture, perceptible already in the preamble to the discourse, is one of confidence in his role as teacher of all mankind:

> [...] oubliant les tems et les Lieux, pour ne songer qu'aux Hommes à qui je parle, je me supposerai dans le Licée d'Athenes, repetant les Leçons de mes Maîtres, ayant les Platons et les Xenocrates pour Juges, et le Genre-humain pour Auditeur.
>
> O Homme, de quelque Contrée que tu sois, quelles que soient tes opinions, écoute; voici ton histoire [...] C'est pour ainsi dire la vie de ton espèce que je vais te décrire. [8]

---

[5] *Discours sur les sciences et les arts*, New York (Modern Language Association of America), 1946, p. 34. Professor George Havens gives in this edition (pp. 34-61) an ample account of the dispute and of the numerous contemporary refutations of the discourse.

[6] The play had been conceived and written much earlier, during Rousseau's stay at Les Charmettes. He took the opportunity of its first publication to write a defense of the First Discourse.

[7] *O. C.* II, p. 973.

[8] *O. C.* III, p. 133.

There is no problem with the reader in the *Discours sur l'iné-galité*, for there is no inner dialogue. His judges are precisely the teachers whose lessons he has learned and is repeating. How could they not approve? Those whom he is really addressing (to be distinguished from the judges, whom he *imagines* himself to be addressing), have no voice: they are auditors. As if upon a forum, Rousseau aims to instruct with his dialectic and to persuade with his eloquence. The ease and self-assurance of his posture, as well as the docility he expects of his reader, can be seen in the mode of presentation: frequent references to the facility of demonstrating his assertions; the prevalent use of the first person plural imperative ("Supposons cette première difficulté vaincue"), indicating an assumption of the immediate acceptance of his dialectic by the reader; most important, the unselfconscious leap —found rather frequently— from supposition to certitude without intermediary demonstration in his reconstruction of primitive man's physical conformation, (for example, Rousseau begins with the locution "*je le supposerai* conformé de tout temps, come je le vois aujourd'hui," passes to "tel qu'*il a dû* sortir des mains de la nature," and finally ends with "*je le vois* se rassasiant sous un chêne"). [9]

The passage from hypothesis to certainty appears to present no problem for Rousseau himself, but will eventually create a problem of first magnitude in his relations with his reader, who will not always be willing to take the necessary leap of faith. Rousseau's subjectivity and typical blurring of the distinction between hypothetical and real have been adequately explored and analyzed. Little attention has been given, however, to these tendencies in terms of the stiff demands that they make on the reader. In the text of the *Discours sur l'inégalité* itself Rousseau gives a helpful account of the psychological basis of his easy progression from supposition to certitude:

> J'avoue que les évenements que j'ai à décrire [i.e., man's evolution from the natural to the social state] ayant pu arriver de plusieurs manières, je ne puis me déterminer sur le choix que par des conjectures; mais,

---

[9] Ibid., pp. 134-135. Emphasis mine.

> outre que ces conjectures deviennent des raisons quand
> elles sont les plus probables qu'on puisse tirer de la
> nature des choses et les seuls moyens qu'on puisse avoir
> de découvrir la verité, les consequences que je veux
> déduire des miennes ne seront point pour cela conjec-
> turales, puisque, sur les principes que je viens d'établir,
> on ne sauroit former aucun autre système qui ne me
> fournisse les mêmes résultats, et dont je ne puisse tirer
> les mêmes conclusions. [10]

In brief, the account of man's social development will be derived
purely from Rousseau's own understanding of the nature of things
and will rest on the validity of the principles he has established
(principles which themselves had earlier appeared as hypotheses).
The important point here is Rousseau's implication that the reader
must accept the writer's beliefs as objective truth. In the last
analysis, the passage quoted has a rhetorical aim, that of shaping
the reader's reaction: any possible objections to the conjectural
nature of Rousseau's arguments are disposed of, and the reader
is assured that there can exist no divergency between the writer
(je) and those who are following his dialectic ("on ne sauroit
former aucun autre système").

The reader thus becomes an automaton, part of an ever-
assenting audience before whom Rousseau may carry on a
monologue. He becomes increasingly a reader of Rousseau's fantasy. One need only look at the next three published works of
Rousseau to see this fantasy operating in full liberty.

*　*　*

LETTRE A M. D'ALEMBERT SUR LES SPECTACLES (1758)

Although ostensibly addressed to d'Alembert, the *Lettre sur
les spectacles* gives little evidence of an overt awareness of an
eventual reader. Rousseau would seem to possess complete
confidence in an immediate, automatic solidarity between himself
and the figure in front of whom he is speaking. Nonetheless, there

---

[10] Ibid., p. 162.

does appear here and there a phenomenon that will assume critical proportions in the *Emile*, i.e., a distinction in the writer's mind between the ideal reader who follows automatically and the "prejudiced" reader who, having been corrupted by opinion, raises objections. Rousseau is in effect addressing two sets of readers in this work, the corrupt Parisians, of whom d'Alembert is the representative, and the simple, virtuous Genevans (such as they existed only in the author's mind) who must be protected from the corrupting influence of the theatre. As yet, Rousseau does not consider the corrupt reader as irremediably damned. He can still be drawn into communion with the author and, like the ideal reader, turned into an automaton. When, for example, the writer momentarily enters the reader's mind in order to wonder aloud what kind of theatre might legitimately exist in a republic ("Mais quels seront enfin les objets de ces Spectacles? Qu'y montrera-t-on?"), the answer is easy and self-assured:

> Rien, si l'on veut. Avec la liberté, partout où règne l'affluence, le bien-être y règne aussi. Plantez au milieu d'une place un piquet couronné de fleurs, rassemblez-y le peuple, et vous aurez une fête. Faites mieux encore: donnez les spectateurs en spectacle; rendez-les acteurs eux-mêmes; faites que chacun se voie et s'aime dans les autres, afin que tous en soient mieux unis. [11]

Rousseau is playing the role of stage-manager for the Play of the Redeemed Society, and there appears no sense of hesitation, no doubt that *all* will want to participate. He frankly and ingenuously uses a series of imperatives. Turning the real, corrupt reader into the ideal reader is up until now a simple matter: one need only present an image of virtue and nature. No voice is heard, inside the witer, objecting that for whatever reasons some might not care to take part in this innocuous kind of "happening." It is not insignificant that this sunny work should end with a fantasy of wish-fulfillment, in which Jean-Jacques, repeating obsessively the "je voudrais que" of rêverie, projects a dazzling

---

[11] *Lettre à Mr. d'Alembert sur les spectacles*, ed. M. Fuchs, Genève (Droz), 1948, pp. 168-169.

image of the world in which he would wish to live and over which he would *rule*.

* * *

Du Contrat social (1762)

In *Du Contrat social*, Rousseau is almost completely encapsuled in his vision of social redemption. Obsessed with his dream, he virtually shunts the reader aside and dreams in public. More than in any of his other works, he conforms here to the traditional image of the humanist rapt in thought, somewhat remote from the world, but nonetheless contemplating the world from his detached vantage point and setting down the results of his contemplation. The serenity of tone is remarkable in comparison with the emotional coloration of the two Discourses and the *Lettre à d'Alembert*. In this, and in the marked preponderance of dialectic over rhetoric, the *Contrat social* is reminiscent of *L'Esprit des Lois* (which it so strongly echoes in substance as well). Our modern conception of the work as incendiary derives from the role it was to play in the various democratic revolutions of the 18th and 19th Centuries, as well as from the unfortunately fragmentary readings done of it. (Firebrand quotations such as the famous "L'homme est né libre, et partout il est dans les fers" seem far less heated in context.) It should be remembered as well that when it appeared, the *Contrat social* was not widely read or discussed, in comparison with other works by Rousseau, who before the revolutionary period was famous largely as the author of the Discourses (confused with each other in the public's mind), *La Nouvelle Héloïse*, and *L'Emile*. The political treatise, a tight fabric of dialectic, was considered by Rousseau's contemporaries to be a "difficult" work.

Rousseau is, in fact, primarily a dialectician in the *Contrat social*, as he will later acknowledge in a note to Book IX of the *Confessions*, speaking of the work as "une entreprise où je voulois mettre uniquement toute la force du raisonnement." [12] As the

---

[12] *O. C.* I, p. 405.

argument proceeds, the author seems to be working out somewhat puzzling and difficult problems, rather in the manner of a geo-metrician elaborating a proof. The opening chapter of the work sets this process in motion:

> L'Homme est né libre, et partout il est dans les fers. Tel se croit le maître des autres, qui ne laisse pas d'être plus esclave qu'eux. Comment ce changement s'est-il fait? Je l'ignore. Qu'est-ce qui peut le rendre légitime? Je crois pouvoir résoudre cette question. [13]

The writer starts with a postulate (universal slavery, described in the closing pages of the Second Discourse), poses a problem (the rectification), and embarks upon the process of reasoning that will lead to the solution. The rest of the work follows in the same line. And although the dialectic frequently involves the use of interrogatives (as in the passage above), it would be improper to refer to them as "rhetorical questions" implying an anticipated response from the reader. Nor are they questions representing an imagined objection by the reader (such as we have seen in his writings). These are, in nearly every case, questions he is asking of *himself*, and represent the next step in the dialectical progression.

Similarly, Rousseau reminds himself of where he stands in his process of reasoning and of where his next step must take him. The prefatory remarks begin with a reminder of his goal: "Je veux chercher si dans l'ordre civil il peut y avoir quelque règle d'administration sûre, en prenant les hommes tels qu'ils sont, et les lois telles qu'elles peuvent être." [14] Or at the beginning of Book II, Ch. 6: "Par le pacte social nous avons donné l'existence et la vie au corps politique: Il s'agit maintenant de lui donner le mouvement et la volonté par la législation." [15] (The wording here suggests a parallel with God, alone and thinking his creation into existence.) And the conclusion of the work appears as a final marker on the road he has travelled:

---

[13] *O. C.* III, p. 351.
[14] Idem.
[15] Ibid., p. 378.

> Après avoir posé les vrais principes du droit politique et tâché de fonder l'Etat sur sa base, il resteroit à l'appuyer par ses relations externes; [...] Mais tout cela forme un nouvel objet trop vaste pour ma courte vue; j'aurois dû la fixer toujours plus près de moi. [16]

Rousseau, then, is looking not at his reader in this work, but at his theorem. Still, he had shown himself capable, in the Second Discourse, of combining brilliant dialectic with extraordinary rhetoric (aimed directly at the reader). How are we to explain his curious lack of concern, in the *Contrat social*, with his reader as a figure to be dealt with, persuaded, swept along? The answer probably lies in the position that this work occupies in the development of Rousseau's political thought and of his relations to Geneva.

As Robert Derathé has pointed out, the author was doubtless already in possession of the core of his political doctrine by 1754. [17] Rousseau himself states in 1762 (letter to Moultou, Jan. 18) that the *Contrat social* was drawn from a larger work to be entitled *Institutions politiques* begun ten years earlier but abandoned. Thus, the work would bear a close relationship to the *Discours sur l'inégalité*, on which Rousseau was working during the same period (approximately 1753-55). In terms of doctrine, it presents the remedy for the catastrophic situation of human society depicted at the end of the Discourse. In tone, it appears as a private, meditative counterpart to the highly public, rhetorical work preceding it. Hence Rousseau would be following one of his typical patterns: an alternation between the frantic attempt to open up lines of communication with the public and the countertendency to withdraw into the private world of his own speculation and fantasy.

Written during the period of Rousseau's proud awareness of his Genevan citizenship (reacquired in 1754) and of his conviction of Geneva's superiority as a model of government, the *Contrat social* is permeated with the author's deep sense of solidarity with his people. In a footnote he speaks of Geneva as "notre ville," [18]

---

[16] Ibid., p. 470.
[17] Ibid., pp. xci-xcviii.
[18] Ibid., p. 362.

and in the preface to Book I he exclaims: "Heureux, toutes les fois que je médite sur les gouvernements, de trouver toujours dans mes recherches de nouvelles raisons d'aimer celui de mon pays." [19] He chooses as his epigraph Latinus' proposal to his subjects, "foederis aequas / Dicamus leges" (*Aeneid*, Book XI), words that eventually bear fruit in bringing the warring Latins into perfect association with their former enemies the Trojans. So Rousseau, addressing *his* men, the citizens of Geneva, will bring an end to universal warfare by setting down the "just laws of association." The *Contrat social* in its entirety might indeed be considered a meditation on the nature of association and on the pathways leading to it. And the feeling for collectivity and solidarity engendered by the meditation is reflected in the rhetorical situation of the work. When Rousseau specifically takes note of the existence of a reader, it is with a serene assumption of solidarity. There is no doubt that the reader will follow the writer, as the people the Lawgiver. (The assumption has, of course, a goodly element of self-delusion in it, since the theorems of the *Contrat social*, unlike those of geometry, are not susceptible to proof positive.) In this work Rousseau rarely apostrophizes the reader, and even when he feels obliged to do so, it is in a soft voice, as to a spiritual brother. We find the familiar footnote admonishing the reader to understand correctly, but expressed here in unusually kindly, confident terms: "Lecteurs attentifs, ne vous pressez pas, je vous prie, de m'accuser de contradiction. Je n'ai pu l'éviter dans les termes, vu la pauvreté de la langue; mais attendez." [20] Again the same tone in the opening paragraph of Book III: "J'avertis le lecteur que ce chapitre doit être lu posément, et que je ne sais pas l'art d'être clair pour qui ne veut pas être attentif." [21] Implied in the parallelism ("être clair... être attentif") is a pact of reciprocity, a contract: if you will read me attentively, I shall be clear to you. There is no question of any problem in comprehension if the reader does his share. Hand in hand, Rousseau and his reader will follow the dialectical path to truth.

✳   ✳   ✳

---

[19] Ibid., p. 351.
[20] Ibid., p. 373.
[21] Ibid., p. 395.

JULIE, OU LA NOUVELLE HÉLOÏSE (1761)

An epistolary novel, lacking a narrator, does not allow for the relatively direct relationship between writer and reader found in other kinds of narrative fiction. We would therefore not expect to find in *La Nouvelle Héloïse* the same evidence of writer-reader relationship as in the works discussed so far. No doubt the choice of a more autonomous, "dramatic" form was dictated at least in part by the intensely personal, private meaning this work had for Rousseau. We know that at a certain point, after the composition of the first four parts, he was determined not to publish the novel. [22] A similar sense of authorial inwardness appears in the First Preface, when Rousseau, wondering to whom the book will be agreeable, answers: "Peut-être à moi seul." [23] The form of the work, then, permits Rousseau to seal himself off in a kind of literary parallel to the blessed solitude of the Ile de Saint-Pierre, a fact that may help explain his predilection for *La Nouvelle Héloïse* among his own writings. It is his private world, into which the reader gazes through one-way glass. Significantly, the Second Preface (written after the composition of the novel, but *before* the First Preface) consists of a dialogue between the author and a reader who has *already* read the novel. The reader is meant, then, to make his first encounter with the work unaccompanied by the author.

Nonetheless, *La Nouvelle Héloïse* provides considerable material for the present study, both directly through consideration of the prefaces and footnotes and, as seen in my Introduction, obliquely through analysis of the handling of the epistolary form.

Both the prefaces and the footnotes (in which Rousseau adopts the rôle of "editor" of the letters) demonstrate the writer's concern, at least after the creative act, with the manner in which he is to be read. Both indicate as well an awareness of the need to educate the reader, who appears in the guise of a man of intelligence and culture, but one whose expectations are based on his experience of the real world and the conventions of current fiction.

---

[22] *O. C.* II, p. L.
[23] Ibid., p. 6.

He is therefore ill-prepared to enter into Rousseau's "monde des chimères." The world of La Nouvelle Héloïse, Rousseau realizes, is bound to seem both referentially and conventionally strange. The author's task in the prefaces and footnotes is to provide a map of the new country the reader will be visiting. He explains oddities of Swiss custom and linguistic usage, elucidates the psychology of the characters (and in general of the inhabitants of the "pays des chimères"), defends literary features such as the "omission" of certain letters, the occurrence of particular stylistic elements, etc.

The explanations are frequently laced, however, with a certain defensive truculence. For example: "Pourquoi l'Editeur laisse-t-il les continuelles répétitions dont cette Lettre est pleine, ainsi que beaucoup d'autres? Par une raison fort simple; c'est qu'il ne se soucie point du tout que ces Lettres plaisent à ceux qui feront cette question." [24] In spite of his assertion, the "editor" (i. e., Rousseau) obviously does care if he bothers to anticipate the reader's question. Here, as in other instances in which Rousseau expresses his supposed unconcern about the reader's possibly unfavorable reaction, the shoulder-shrugging betrays an awareness of the exasperating problems involved in the attempt to convey a specific message or vision and to have it understood exactly as intended. Seen from an historical point of view, Rousseau undoubtedly found himself in the same awkward position as the other writers of his generation, born and bred during the high period of neo-classicism, writing for a reading public whose taste was normative and rigid, and attempting withal to do something new. One need only leaf through the literary reviews of the period 1730-1770 to know what lofty, self-assured carping about language, subject, and treatment of subject the more original authors had to put up with. Rousseau must surely have understood that the literary conservatives would inevitably misunderstand and ridicule his work (as Voltaire did). The statement of independence quoted above is, in this light, a thoroughly apt response to historical circumstance. The very terms in which Rousseau chooses to couch his unconcern are historically charged. He claims not to care

---

[24] Ibid., p. 632.

whether the letters "please" the reader. The term and notion, essential to neo-classic esthetics and literary doctrine, infuriated Rousseau, who saw in this rôle of the writer as one who "pleases" the reader one more manifestation of social corruption, through which the writer, by rights a truthteller, is made the pimp of the moneyed and powerful. Hence the laconically scornful tone of the disclaimer.

Still, the strength and persistency of Rousseau's assertions, throughout the prefaces and footnotes, of total unconcern for the reader's judgment suggest that in addition to the normal reaction to historical circumstance there is a certain amount of personal defensiveness involved. Rousseau's extreme sensitivity to adverse opinion is well-known. *La Nouvelle Héloïse* is, as we have seen, an artistic representation of the author's dream world. Any negative response to it will be in effect a condemnation and rejection of his private vision of truth and virtue. The easiest way to protect himself from this response is to declare in advance that the critic is unworthy of notice. The negative reader becomes an un-reader, like the un-persons of certain modern Rousseauistic political ideologies. But at the same time, by posting in advance his scornful dismissal of this hypothetical reader, Rousseau exerts pressure on the actual reader of his novel to distinguish himself by his greater cleverness and understanding, which will permit him to recognize the previously unknown truth placed before him.

One sees a similar strategy at work in the prefaces. A refrain runs through them: you, reader, cannot discern whether this work is truth or fiction. Rousseau teases the reader, and glories in his own independence and power. It is as if, having provided the reader with a glimpse of the land of enchantment, Rousseau protects the privileged territory (and himself, since it is his homeland) by confusing the reader, who is tempted to believe the whole vison a fiction but who cannot break the spell. For Rousseau, it is of the utmost importance that the world of Julie exist. His sense of the "reality of the imaginary" (to borrow Marc Eigeldinger's formula) [25] will not, however, be shared by his

---

[25] *Jean-Jacques Rousseau et la réalité de l'imaginaire*, Neuchâtel (La Bâconnière), 1962. Professor Eigeldinger studies Rousseau's tendency to deal with the imaginary as if it were real.

realistic, pragmatic, conventional reader, who will reject and ridicule if he is allowed to touch the enchantment and see it disappear. Yet, as we shall see, Rousseau cannot lie outright to his reader, and therefore must equivocate. And his equivocation is a supreme rhetorical achievement: the little dance he performs succeeds in confusing the fiction-reality issue far more effectively than the conventional claim of documentary reality could conceivably have done.

*   *   *

Rousseau's fantasy of his relationship with his reader as represented in the prefaces to his novel might stand as a faithful image of his rhetorical posture during the entire period under discussion in this chapter. As with his youthful phallic exhibitions in Turin, he exposes his doctrine, but at a safe distance and with a convenient escape route available. He senses that there exists an "other-mind problem," and that the capacities of the real reader to understand are limited, but keeps the uncomfortable recognition at bay through evasive tactics: the nourishment of a fantasy of a perfect reader, with whom he can enjoy complete solidarity; the simple rejection of the uncooperative reader; and the exclusion of the reader through adoption of a form in which he cannot be addressed directly. Rousesau seems to show little interest in establishing, through contact with his reader-figure, the kind of dialectic that opens up the closed circuit of the mind and facilitates change in perception and comprehension. In other terms, Rousseau is following the procedures typical of the imaginative writer, who is in fact free to work with a reader-figure possessing a relatively low reality ratio, since he aims primarily at procuring the reader's comprehension of the *thusness* of the message. Roussaeu, however, thought of himself not as a purveyor of fictions, but as a teacher of truth, i. e., as one who proposes to gain the reader's assent to the *rightness* of the message. In matters involving truth, the process of testing-out and corroboration through another mind is essential, and it is this process that Rousseau has in fact been avoiding.[26] He was content to dream, hoping to have his dream accepted as reality.[27] And his genius was such that to an extraordinary extent he did succeed in imposing his dream upon the world. His triumph, however, will have a price attached to it in terms of miscomprehension and self-torture. As in Turin, he cannot hope to elude forever the man with the great moustache and the sword. The direct encounter with the real reader, the public, provided by the publication of the *Emile*, will put an end to the easy solutions.

---

[26] Perhaps the fundamental difference between Rousseau and Diderot, whose thought and attitudes show so many affinities, lies in precisely this area. Diderot's avowed method in writing is to imagine himself addressing a friend or acquaintance, and to attempt to imagine (with moderate good faith) his interlocutor's reaction. His thought is basically dialogic, while Rousseau's is self-containedly dialectical. Diderot described with brilliance this particular quality of Rousseau's mind in the *Salon de 1765*, perceiving both the internally logical, the solipsistic, and the persuasive aspects of his erstwhile friend's writings: "J'aime les fanatiques; non pas ceux qui vous présentent une formule absurde de croyance, et qui, vous portant le poignard à la gorge, vous crient: 'Signe ou meurs;' mais bien ceux qui, fortement épris de quelque goût particulier et innocent, ne voient plus rien qui lui soit comparable, le défendent de toute leur force; vont dans les maisons et les rues, non la lance, mais le syllogisme en arrêt, sommant et ceux qui passent et ceux qui sont arrêtés, de convenir de leur absurdité, ou de la supériorité des charmes de leur Dulcinée sur toutes les créatures du monde. Ils sont plaisants, ceux-ci. Ils m'amusent; ils m'étonnent quelquefois. Quand par hasard ils ont rencontré la vérité, ils l'exposent avec une énergie qui brise et renverse tout. Dans le paradoxe, accummulant images sur images, appelant à leur secours toutes les puissances de l'éloquence, les expressions figurées, les comparaisons hardies, les tours, les mouvements; s'adressant au sentiment, à l'imagination; attaquant l'âme et sa sensibilité par toutes sortes d'endroits, le spectacle de leurs efforts est encore beau. Tel est Jean-Jacques Rousseau [...]" (*Œuvres complètes*, Paris [Garnier], 1876, vol. X, pp. 416-417).

[27] In a curious footnote to the *Emile* (Paris, Garnier, 1961, p. 109), Rousseau will reflect on the highly subjective nature of contemporary philosophy (in spite of the philosophers' claims to the contrary), adding: "On me dira que je rêve aussi; j'en conviens: mais ce que les autres n'ont garde de faire, je donne mes rêves pour des rêves, laissant chercher au lecteur s'ils ont quelque chose d'utile aux gens éveillés." There is a certain amount of bad faith in this assertion. If Rousseau presents his writings as dreams (which is debatable), he does so with the conviction that he dreams the truth, since he carries nature and truth within him. Moreover, if he does "let the reader discern" whether his dreams contain something useful, it is only after the act of writing and the fact of publication. As a writer, he doesn't allow the reader any choice at all, except the initial choice of reading or refusing to read.

Chapter II

THE REFRACTORY READER

Rousseau was as sensitive and suspicious towards his public as towards his friends, and any hint of hostility or miscomprehension on the part of his readers set off fierce reactions. These reactions were in turn bound to influence his gestures and attitudes as a writer. We have valuable evidence of Rousseau's immediate response to an unfavorable reading in the brief *Réponse à une lettre anonyme* (Oct. 15, 1758). The anonymous letter reads as follows (in Rousseau's transcription of it):

> Des gens de loix, qui estiment, etc., M. Rousseau, ont été surpris et affligés de son opinion dans sa lettre à M. d'Alembert sur le Tribunal des Maréchaux de france. Un Citoyen aussi éclairé que M. Rousseau n'ignore pas qu'on ne peut justement devoiler aux yeux de la nation les fautes de la Legislation. Les Philosophes sont faits pour éclairer le Ministère, le détromper de ses erreurs, et respecter ses fautes. De plus, M. Rousseau ne nous paroit pas raisonner en politique lorsqu'il admet dans un état une Autorité supérieure à l'Autorité souveraine, ou du moins indépendante d'elle. Il ne se rappelloit pas dans ce moment le sentiment de Grotius, adopté par les Encyclopédistes ses confrères. Le tems nous empêche d'exposer plusieurs autres objections qui exigeroient une conversation qui priveroit M. Rousseau d'un temps précieux pour lui et pour le public.

Rousseau's reply consists of a testy, lofty, satirical "réfutation suivie." The significant aspect of the reply, aside from the evident irritation motivating it (Rousseau despised anonymous writings), is the writer's clear effort to dissociate himself as a *person* from this group of critical readers, or to dissociate them from him. He notes that because of their difference in nationality he is not writing for them. He claims not to understand the word "ministère": no such office exists in Geneva. He claims to be independent of the "autorité souveraine" to which they refer. Above all, he asserts the irrelevance of their opinion by rejecting them as his readers: "si vous me lisez, ce n'est pas ma faute"; "comme il n'est pas bon que nous nous entendions mieux, nous ferons bien de n'en pas discuter." [1] The lines of communication are cut.

It is important to understand the nature and motivation of this withdrawal, for it will come to dominate Rousseau's attitude towards his readers to a point where he will finally be forced to conceive of himself as having no readers at all. Possibly Rousseau's behavior towards his friends will cast some light on his behavior towards his reader. Completely trusting, in childlike fashion, up to the point where some imagined or real incomprehension, slight, criticism, or gesture of malice intervenes, Rousseau then consigns the erstwhile friend to the category of the *méchants,* with whom communication is both impossible and undesirable. The break with Diderot is typical of this pattern. While doubtless guilty, in a minor way, of inattentiveness and indiscretion, Diderot surely did not deserve (and must have been stupefied by) the dramatic, irrevocable repudiation in the preface to the *Lettre à d'Alembert*. Yet Rousseau never seems to have had second thoughts about the repudiation, nor ever to have considered the situation as admitting of any ambiguity or complexity.

The same pattern of total rejection is seen in his relations with his readers. As soon as a particular reader or group of readers misunderstands, ridicules, or (through inattentive reading) slights a book or even a passage by Rousseau, the author dissolves the relationship, refusing henceforth to write for him or for them. The reader has proved that he is not the reader Rousseau had in mind, who alone can understand him (and who alone is worthy of seeing the enchanted garden). The problem created by this

---

[1] *Correspondance générale,* Paris (Colin), 1925, t. 4, pp. 85-89.

repudiation is considerable. As the circle or Rousseau's "proper" readers narrows, the question of whom to address becomes ever more acute, as does, indeed, a feeling of panic at his inability to convince the world of his truth. Rousseau was never to lack a reading public, far from it. But public renown and even acclaim was of little consequence to him in comparison with the desire to be perfectly understood and completely accepted.

❋   ❋   ❋

EMILE (1762)

The conflict between desire for an ideal reader and recognition of the limited capacities of the real reader reaches critical proportions in *Emile ou de l'Education* (1762) and in the subsequent attacks upon and defenses of the work. The moment is crucial for Rousseau both as a public figure and as a writer. At the beginning of 1762, he was at the height of his public career. He had enjoyed a full year of adulation following the publication early in 1761 of *La Nouvelle Héloïse*. He had the friendship and patronage of the powerful Luxembourg family and of Malesherbes, the head of the censorship branch of the police. By the middle of June, 1762, he was a fugitive. The *Emile* had been condemned in Paris, as it was to be in various other European capitals, including Geneva. It will be eight years before the ex-Citizen's wanderings will be over and he will once more settle in Paris (still officially under warrant for arrest), there to finish his days. Thus, the publication of the *Emile* constitutes a dramatic turning point in Rousseau's life. This aspect of his personal biography is not, however, of primary concern here. The relevant question is rather the extent to which we can, in examining the *Emile* and Rousseau's defenses of it, discern a change in his relationship to his reader. In this area, too, as we shall see, this work is pivotal, closing Rousseau's great period of public teaching and announcing a new orientation towards personal exploration and revelation that will characterize in various ways the rest of his writings.

❋   ❋   ❋

In writing the *Emile*, Rousseau has more than one reader in mind. He is addressing the young preceptor: "Jeune instituteur, je vous prêche un art difficile." [2] This awareness reflects that aspect of the *Emile* consisting of a pedagogical manual, perhaps the least important and least interesting aspect of the work, which is in fact Rousseau's "essay on man." He is also addressing humanity, as in the First Discourse. Here, however, the tone is not generally forensic, but alternately Montaignean (with the typical equalizing usage of "nous") and Orphic. Rousseau sings to men the melody of truth and brings them a message of divine inspiration: "Hommes, soyez humains, c'est votre premier devoir." [3] And he is in addition addressing the contemporary reading public, this time not just the Genevans (as in the *Contrat social*) but all of his contemporaries. The *Emile* must have been particularly important to Rousseau (witness his paranoid fantasies about the theft and adulteration of the manuscript), for he is not content here to sit inside his conveniently encapsuled world, as he had been in the three preceding works. He makes an attempt to communicate with the real reader, the spokesmen and bulwarks of contemporary "civilization," running the gamut from atheists and libertines to Jansenists.

It is primarily this last group of readers —the contemporary reading public— that poses a problem for Rousseau, and with whom we see him wrestle in the *Emile*. The anticipated objection appears with considerable frequency: "Que de voix vont s'élever contre moi! J'entends de loin les clameurs de cette fausse sagesse"; "vous me direz que [...] on m'objectera que [...]," etc. Or in references to his own peculiar way of seeing things (for he had by this time become aware that others thought him paradoxical), he will make remarks such as: "Depuis longtemps ils me voient dans le pays des chimères; moi, je les vois toujours dans le pays des préjugés." [4] Examples of the author's awareness of this "hostile" public abound, occurring on practically every page, and there would be little point in cataloguing them.

---

[2] *Emile*, p. 120.
[3] Ibid., p. 62.
[4] Ibid., p. 304.

There is a particular tension in his relationship with this set of readers. In the earlier sections (approximately the first two books), he will anticipate an objection, refute the objection, and then pass on to a reconciliation with the now-convinced reader, finishing often with a lyrical, Orphic repetition of what is now seen not merely as an individual assertion but rather as a universally accepted truth. The terminal stage of this progression resembles the "feast of harmony and reconciliation" that recurs throughout Rousseau's works as an idyllic vision. (It is the rhetorical analogue of the "retour" designated by Starobinski as one of Rousseau's obsessive psychological motifs.) [5] This mechanism (present already in the First Discourse) is based on an assumption that guides Rousseau's writing up to, but excluding, the *Rêveries du promeneur solitaire:* if he tells his truth with conviction, he cannot fail to convince the reader and to make the reader share his vision of things. Rousseau himself gives a striking description of the mechanism in a brief passage in Book IV of the *Emile* (the "Profession de foi du vicaire savoyard"). The young man, a somewhat fictionalized version of the young Rousseau, says of the vicar:

> Le bon prêtre avait parlé avec véhémence; il était ému, je l'étais aussi. Je croyais entendre le divin Orphée chanter les premiers hymnes, et apprendre aux hommes le culte des dieux. Cependant je voyais une foule d'objections à lui faire: je n'en fis pas une, parce qu'elles etaient moins solides qu'embarrassantes, et que la persuasion était pour lui. À mesure qu'il me parlait selon sa conscience, la mienne semblait me confirmer ce qu'il m'avait dit. [6]

The objections here are silent, just as the reader's are (it is Rousseau who gives voice to them), and the pattern of assertion, objection, and reconciliation through a magical, intuitive kind of persuasion is the same. The convinceable young man stands in the same relationship to the vicar as the convinceable reader of the *Emile* to Rousseau. [7]

---

5 *Jean-Jacques Rousseau,* pp. 151-168.
6 *Emile,* p. 359.
7 There is additional evidence of a strong identification between Rousseau and his Vicar in the manner in which they address their respective

Rousseau is evidently involved in a sleight of hand in his use of this mechanism. He seems at first, in his anticipation of the objection, to be speaking to the real reader, the "other mind" that can and will question the writer's assertions. But this reader, whose voice is audible to Rousseau, undergoes a magical change into the convinceable reader, Rousseau's creature. This creature, the ideal reader, has entered into the "contract" mentioned earlier, a kind of "contrat littéraire" analogous to Rousseau's social and pedagogical contracts.

As with the social and pedagogical pacts, the fundamental notion in the "contrat littéraire" is, as we have seen, that of reciprocity. "If you will read me properly, I shall bring you my truth (which equals *the* truth)." Although this contract is nowhere spelled out explicitly in Rousseau's writings, the existence of a set of conventions between himself and his reader is mentioned

---

reader or listener. The Vicar expresses himself as follows: "Mon enfant, n'attends de moi ni des discours savants ni de profonds raisonnements. Je ne suis pas un grand philosophe, et je me soucie peu de l'être. Mais j'ai quelquefois du bon sens, et j'aime toujours la vérité" (p. 320). Earlier in the work, Rousseau had made virtually the same disclaimer to his reader: "Lecteurs, souvenez-vous que celui qui vous parle n'est ni un savant ni un philosophe, mais un homme simple, ami de la vérité, sans parti, sans système" (p. 107). If the identification Vicar-Rousseau is valid, then the sense of the Vicar's relationship to the young man would apply to Rousseau's relationship to the reader. The Vicar's words are, in this light, extremely revealing: "J'épancherai dans votre sein [...] tous les sentiments de mon cœur. Vous me verrez, sinon tel que je suis, au moins tel que je me vois moi-même. Quand vous aurez reçu mon entière profession de foi, quand vous connaîtrez l'état de mon âme, vous saurez pourquoi je m'estime heureux, et, si vous pensez comme moi, ce que vous avez à faire pour l'être [...] Je ne veux pas argumenter avec vous, ni même tenter de vous convaincre; il me suffit de vous exposer ce que je pense dans la simplicité de mon cœur. Consultez le vôtre durant mon discours; c'est tout ce que je vous demande. Si je me trompe, c'est de bonne foi; cela suffit pour que mon erreur ne me soit point imputée à crime: quand vous vous tromperiez de même, il y aurait peu de mal à cela. Si je pense bien, la raison nous est commune, et nous avons le même intérêt à l'écouter; pourquoi ne penseriez-vous pas comme moi?" (pp. 319-320). I shall deal later, in relation to the *Confessions,* with Rousseau's desire to present himself to the reader as a model and to turn the reader into another Rousseau. The Vicar's words clearly show this motivation, culminating as they do in the wheedling question "Pourquoi ne penseriez-vous pas comme moi?" The reader will "set himself" according to Rousseau, and the two shall continue to exist as two identical, synchronized time-pieces. This is one way of appropriating the reader, making him the ideal reader.

in the *Emile*,[8] and their terms may be deduced from various statements by Rousseau concerning what he expects of his reader and what his reader may in turn expect from him. Rousseau, a latter-day Orpheus, will impart wisdom and truth and a plan for regeneration. The reader in turn must read with good will and in good faith; he must share Rousseau's preoccupations; he must be patient, for the writer cannot say everything simultaneously; he must allow the author complete freedom to proceed as he wishes (to reminisce, for example, about his childhood, or to include lengthy and admittedly irrelevant digressions); above all, the reader must bring to his reading powers of intuition that will permit him to understand that which is imperfectly communicated, or even left unsaid.

The final stipulation amounts at times to an expectation of clairvoyance on the reader's part. Students of Rousseau are familiar with his obsession with transparency, or unmediated communication. Understandably, this obsession operates strongly in the area of verbal communication: Rousseau mistrusts words as mediators of significance precisely because, as mediators, they cannot fail to obscure communication. His notion of the imperfection of language is clearly formulated in the *Lettre à Christophe de Beaumont:* "Le langage humain n'est pas assez clair. Dieu lui même, s'il daignoit nous parler dans nos langues, ne nous diroit rien sur quoi l'on ne pût disputer."[9] Much consideration is given in the *Emile* to various problems involved in verbal communication, and always with the anticipation that words will not convey meaning properly. (The famous criticism of "Le Corbeau et le renard" in Book II centers on this point, and it is instructive to see how extreme, almost perverse, a *mis*comprehension of the poem Rousseau expects from the child.)

Now, the only solution to the problem that arises from the *necessity* of using words is an act of faith: the writer will trust the reader to understand what is meant in spite of the inevitable obscurity of language. Rousseau acts consciously on this assumption in the *Emile:* "S'il faut tout vous dire, ne me lisez

---

[8] Ibid., p. 118.

[9] *Jean-Jacques Rousseau, citoyen de Genève, à Christophe de Beaumont* [...], Amsterdam, 1763, pp. 110-111.

point." [10] His faith in the reader's ability to grasp his meaning intuitively appears in the footnote appended to his unusual use of the adjective *native* in the sense of "original": "J'emploie ce mot dans une acception italienne, faute de lui trouver un synonyme en français. Si j'ai tort, peu m'importe, pourvu qu'on m'entende." [11] (Yet the act of pointing out the unusual meaning to the reader would indicate a certain doubt as to the reader's ability to understand.) Similarly, in another footnote, this one dealing with the impossibility of using a word always with the same definition, he affirms his trust in the reader's ability to discern the precise meaning in each instance through context. [12]

Rousseau's understanding of the nature of language was remarkably modern (i. e., in advance of the rationalistic grammar of the period), and his call for a certain effort of intuition on the readers part is surely justified up to a point. But with his habitual insistence on pushing everything to the absolute (at the same time his strength and his weakness), he occasionally wants his reader to know things not even hinted at. Here, the intervention of the real reader, operating outside of Rousseau's set of conventions, clearly reveals the nature and depth of the problem created by this expectancy. There certainly exists no lack of raw material for a study on the reactions to Rousseau's writings during his lifetime and his own response to these reactions. A thorough study of this question would require many years of research. Luckily, there exists in the case of the *Emile* a delimited, exemplary field of study, the interaction between Rousseau and Jean-Henri-Samuel Formey.

Shortly after the publication of the *Emile*, Formey, a German-born scholar of French Huguenot parentage, published an *Anti-Emile* (a "réfutation suivie") and an *Emile chrétien* (nothing more than an expurgated version of Rousseau's work). Rousseau was understandably enraged, and replied pungently to Formey's commentary in footnotes to a 1765 edition of the *Emile*. Now, Formey's reading of the *Emile* is particularly valuable for the present discussion, for he was not only a real, contemporary

---

[10] *Emile*, p. 145.
[11] Ibid., p. 177.
[12] Ibid., p. 104.

reader, but also a reader of considerable intelligence and learning. As a defender of throne and altar, he considered himself an opponent of the *philosophes*, although, as was the case with many of the supposed opponents, he was in fact deeply imbued with their ideas and in tacit agreement with their perspectives. His reading of the *Emile* is careful [13] and perceptive, and he is sufficiently openminded to lavish praise on certain sections of the work. Where he misunderstands or criticizes Rousseau, he generally has some justification. How many of Rousseau's contemporaries were capable of accepting as valid and useful the self-avowed imaginings of a visionary?

In the criticism of interest here, Formey picks up the episode of the mountebank ("bateleur") in Book III. In this episode, the Tutor accompanies Emile to a fair, where they watch a mountebank attract little toy ducks in a bowl of water by holding a piece of bread near their beaks. Emile is intrigued, and that evening he figures out the trick (with the usual hidden manipulation of the Tutor): the mountebank had placed a magnet in the piece of bread, and the ducks beaks were made of iron. Emile decides to trick the trickster by hiding a magnet of his own in a piece of bread and thus accomplishing the same feat the next day at the fair. All goes as expected, and the mountebank, thoroughly discomfited, invites the pair back for the following day's exhibition. Emile's vanity is aroused, and it is a dangerous moment in his moral development. But the next day, when he and his tutor return to the fair, he cannot control the ducks: they turn tail to his bread. The mountebank, on the other hand, seems to be able to direct them according to his will (we find out later that this time he had an accomplice with a magnet hidden under the table). The Tutor and Emile return home in silence. The next morning,

---

[13] His carefulness irritated Rousseau. When Formey points out, for example, that "Le Corbeau et le renard" is not, as Rousseau had put it, the first but the second of La Fontaine's fables, Rousseau corrects himself with testy irony in a footnote: "C'est la seconde, et non la première, comme l'a très bien remarqué M. Formey" (p. 111). Had Rousseau really accepted the correction (the intervention of another mind), he would merely have corrected his own faulty text; instead, he attempts to hold Formey up to ridicule as an example of the petty reader. Rousseau sees his intervention as an intrusion into his ideal rhetorical situation, and repels the attack.

the mountebank appears at the door and delivers a judicious and rather humiliating sermon to Emile and, especially, to the Tutor, the main theme of which is respect for other people and their trade. "Il part et nous laisse tous deux très confus," Rousseau tells us.

Now, Formey ridiculed the wise discourse of the mountebank, a Socrates who, he says, could exist only in "le monde des Emiles." Rousseau, in turn, comments at some length on Formey's criticism:

> Le spirituel M. Formey n'a pu supposer que cette petite scène était arrangée, et que le bateleur était instruit du rôle qu'il avait à faire; car c'est en effet ce que je n'ai point dit. Mais combien de fois, en revanche, ai-je déclaré que je n'écrivais point pour les gens à qui il fallait tout dire! [14]

> Ai-je dû supposer quelque lecteur assez stupide pour ne pas sentir dans cette réprimande un discours dicté mot à mot par le gouverneur pour aller à ses vues? A-t-on dû me supposer assez stupide moi-même pour donner naturellement ce langage à un bateleur? Je croyais avoir fait preuve au moins du talent assez médiocre de faire parler les gens dans l'esprit de leur état. Voyez la fin de l'alinéa suivant. [This is a reference to a seemingly unrelated comment concerning the approaching necessity of changing the kind of relationship the Tutor will have with Emile, and ending with the remark: "Il faut tout prévoir, et tout prévoir de fort loin."] [15]

Rousseau concludes by asking: "N'était-ce pas tout dire pour tout autre que M. Formey?"

Without the help of Rousseau's footnotes, very few readers would, I suspect, have the slightest realization that the Socratic lesson delivered by the mountebank had been dictated by the Tutor, or that the Tutor had anything at all to do with the course of events. Of the twenty to thirty readers of the *Emile* whom I have questioned on this point, *not one* had failed to be amazed by Rousseau's tardy revelation in the footnote, *not one* had

---

[14] Ibid., p. 193.
[15] Ibid., p. 196.

"intuited" the Tutor's intervention. In our defense, I would point out that Rousseau is indeed not known for his ability to adapt language to the individual. Quite the contrary, his characters tend to sound very much like himself. Furthermore, whereas in a number of other instances involving this kind of secret manipulation by the Tutor Rousseau specifically informs the reader of this manipulation, in the present instance almost nothing would lead us to suspect the presence of the Tutor's hand, and several notations would seem specifically to *absolve* the Tutor from any connivance. (For example, the "il *nous* laisse *tous deux* très confus" quoted above implies a clear moral fault on the part of the Tutor as well as Emile.) True enough, the author does counsel the young preceptor reading his book to watch carefully for the first movement of vanity in his pupil, adding: "Si vous savez en *faire sortir ainsi* l'humiliation, les disgrâces, soyez sûr qu'il n'en reviendra de longtemps un second" (my emphasis). This comment elicits in turn a triumphant footnote in the 1765 edition:

> Cette humiliation, ces disgrâces sont donc de ma façon, et non pas de celle du bateleur. Puisque M. Formey voulait de mon vivant s'emparer de mon livre [a reference to the *Emile chrétien*], et le faire imprimer sans autre façon que d'en ôter mon nom pour y mettre le sien, il devait du moins prendre la peine, je ne dis pas de le composer, mais de le lire. [16]

In Rousseau's mind, the expression "faire sortir ainsi" gives the whole manipulation away, and any reader who misses this more than subtle hint "hasn't read his book." A reading, for Rousseau, is perfect or non-existent.

The terms in which Rousseau couches his persiflage of Formey reveal the nature of the desired relationship with the reader. The reader is meant to "feel" *(sentir)* that the discourse has been dictated by the Tutor. A form of total enlightenment is supposed to derive from the single comment about "preparing everything in advance": "N'était-ce pas *tout dire?*" And the writer attempts to set up a complicity of contempt with his second round of readers, who must have understood properly (i.e., as Rousseau

---

[16] Ibid., p. 197.

understood). He carefully separates *all* other readers from the opaque, the intractable Formey. It is a clever psychological strategy, mixing threat and flattery: the reader is given the option of being stupid with Formey or lucid with Rousseau.

Yet the reader's "misreading" is unquestionably justified. The ideal reader, with whom Rousseau is working, and who has subscribed to the "contrat littéraire," understands the passage. The real reader, Formey (and doubtless nearly everyone else who has read this passage), does not. He expects Rousseau to tell him what he needs to know.

✿ ✿ ✿

In a sense, Rousseau was a prisoner of his motto: *Vitam impendere vero*. His excursions into the world of illusion, while very much part of his character, are never entirely successful or enduring, and on some level he always maintains contact with reality (hence, for example, the death of Julie and the dissolution of the ideal society at the end of *La Nouvelle Héloïse*). No doubt he was aware of the unreality of his ideal reader and of the illusory nature of a rhetorical situation set up for his own convenience. The *Emile* shows Rousseau awakening from his dream of the perfect relationship with the ideal reader, or at least returning from the illusion of an exact correspondence between ideal and real reader.

We have seen Rousseau's capacity for drawing his imaginary reader's vision into perfect alignment with his own. This pattern, particularly strong in the first two books of the *Emile*, tends to weaken as the work progresses, giving place to a new pattern which, although of infrequent occurrence, is invested with considerable feeling. The author, while still anticipating the reader's objections, now begins to foresee as well his own *inability* to convince the reader. Thus the ideal reader gives way to the real reader, whose existence Rousseau acknowledges with some bitterness:

> J'avance, attiré par la force des choses, mais sans m'en imposer sur les jugements des lecteurs. Depuis longtemps ils me voient dans le pays des chimères; moi,

> je les vois toujours dans le pays des préjugés. En m'écar-
> tant si fort des opinions vulgaires, je ne cesse de les
> avoir présentes à mon esprit: je les examine, je les médite,
> non pour les suivre ni pour les fuir, mais pour les peser
> à la balance du raisonnement. Toutes les fois qu'il me
> force à m'écarter d'elles, instruit par l'expérience, je
> me tiens déjà pour dit qu'ils ne m'imiteront pas: je sais
> que, s'obstinant à n'imaginer possible que ce qu'ils voient,
> ils prendront le jeune homme que je figure pour un être
> imaginaire et fantastique. [17]

A similar note appears in the preface (written after completion
of the text itself): "On croira moins lire un traité d'éducation que
les rêveries d'un visionnaire sur l'éducation. Qu'y faire? Ce n'est
pas sur les idées d'autrui que j'écris; c'est sur les miennes. Je ne
vois point comme les autres hommes; il y a longtemps qu'on me
l'a reproché." [18] Further on: "Lecteur, j'aurai beau faire, je sens
bien que vous et moi ne verrons jamais mon Emile sous les
mêmes traits." [19] Still later: "Vous n'imaginez pas comment, à
vingt ans, Emile peut être si docile. Que nous pensons différem-
ment!" [20]

As the desired unity of vision with the ideal reader breaks
down under the impact of experience (as Rousseau specifically
notes), the use of the "nous solidaire," so frequent in the first
books, gives way to a "nous" designating the restrictive community
of Rousseau and the "jeune instituteur," who, presumably not
belonging to the world of "ces messieurs-là," is still receptive to
the truth, still capable of reading Rousseau properly.

Rousseau's tension with his reader, his growing sense of malaise
in his relation with him, are explicable even without recourse
to the evident medical explanation. (In any case, the onset of
his first paranoid crisis, due in part to uremic toxicity, dates from
November, 1761, i.e., after the manuscript had been sent off to
the publisher.) First of all, Rousseau had for some time been
aware of (and even gloried in) the gulf separating him from
certain segments of the public, both the *philosophes* and the

---

[17] Ibid., p. 304.
[18] Ibid., p. 2.
[19] Ibid., p. 390.
[20] Ibid., p. 414.

representatives of the established order. But although he enjoyed renown, protection, and (in many quarters) adulation, he could not help, given his particular character, resenting bitterly the miscomprehension and hostility of even a limited number of readers. Reality could hardly measure up to his dream, the dream of the messiah. He could not have been unaware, either, that what he had to say in the *Emile,* particularly in Book IV, was bound to elicit a storm of controversy. We should not be taken in by his customary show of naiveté, his bewilderment at the fears expressed by his friends, his protestations concerning the evident goodness and soundness of his doctrine. His obsessive fantasies involving malevolent plots against the publication of the *Emile,* or of its adulteration by the Jesuits, provide far more accurate an indication of his true state of mind at the time, and of his anxiety about his relationship with the public. He knew that the role of prophet, even outside one's own country, is not an easy one.

Still, this does not entirely explain why there should appear signs of a change in his relation to his reader within the *Emile* itself, a change that seems to have occurred *during* the writing of the work. An additional hypothesis is available, however. In writing the *Emile,* the work in which he presents most openly and fully his doctrine and his message of redemption, Rousseau may well have felt uneasy and even slightly guilty in his role as purveyor of truth. Towards the end of his life, in the Quatrième Promenade of the *Rêveries,* he examines at length the question of truth, in its general dimensions and as a personal problem for himself. After several attempts at self-justification, he finally admits his guilt:

> Je ne sens pourtant pas mon cœur assez content de ces distinctions pour me croire tout à fait irrépréhensible. En pesant avec tant de soin ce que je devois aux autres, ai-je assez examiné ce que je devois à moi-même? S'il faut être juste pour autrui, il faut être vrai pour soi, c'est un hommage que l'honnête homme doit rendre à sa propre dignité. Quand la stérilité de ma conversation me forçoit d'y suppléer par d'innocentes fictions, j'avois tort, parce qu'il ne faut point pour amuser autrui s'avilir soi-même; *et quand entraîné par le plaisir d'écrire, j'ajoutois à des choses réelles des ornements inventés*

j'avois plus de tort encore parce qu'orner la vérité par des fables c'est en effet la defigurer.

Mais ce qui me rend plus inexcusable encore est la dévise que j'avois choisie. Cette devise m'obligeoit plus que tout autre homme à une profession plus étroite de la vérité, et il ne suffisoit pas que je lui sacrifiasse par tout mon intérêt et mes penchans, il falloit lui sacrifier aussi ma foiblesse et mon naturel timide. Il falloit avoir le courage et la force d'*être vrai toujours en toute occasion et qu'il ne sortit jamais ni fiction ni fable d'une bouche et d'une plume qui s'étoit particulierement consacrée à la vérité.* Voila ce que j'aurois dû me dire en prenant cette fiére devise, et me répéter sans cesse tant que j'osai la porter. [21]

To what extent was Rousseau, in the *Emile,* fulfilling the stipulation of his motto? To what extent was he living up to his part of the contract with the reader, i.e., bringing him the pure truth? Telling the truth is not so simple an enterprise, as he himself recognizes at the beginning of the Promenade quoted above.

Rousseau admits in several passages of the *Emile* (one of which we have seen) that he is merely setting forth his "visions." His advantage, he claims, lies in his *knowing* that they are visions. And he might well have defended himself by asserting that *his* visions stemmed from a true understanding of nature, just as in the Second Discourse he had proved to his own satisfaction that his conjectures were equivalent to the truth. What would be less easy to defend is the admixture of fiction and distortion in some of the material he presents. One instance is particularly telling: the version of an experience at the monastic hospice in Turin where Rousseau underwent his conversion to Catholicism in 1728.

In the *Emile,* we are given the tale of a high-minded young man who is subjected to the outrageous advances of a man of importance and power in the hospice. When in an access of rage and indignation the young man seeks assistance in dealing with this cruel victimization, he meets only indifference, laughter, or evil counsel. Only through the imprudent but courageous aid of a young priest does he succeed in escaping from the cursèd

---

[21] *O. C.* I, pp. 1038-9. Emphasis mine.

monastery. [22] (Rousseau seems here to be influenced by the *roman noir*, which had already made its appearance early in the century —witness the story of Sylvie in Chasles's *Illustres Françoises*— and the elements of which had already started to appear on the stage in the 1740's.)

The version we find of the same episode in the *Confessions*, only a few years later, is quite different. A Moorish proselyte of no importance whatever, and who apparently made a living through his repeated conversions, had befriended the young Rousseau in the hospice and then attempted to make indecent advances. The boy was shocked and disgusted, and (as he puts it) naively went about recounting the event. No one seemed to care very much about it, except for an old serving-woman who muttered a few curses in Piedmontese against the Moor. The superior of the hospice told Rousseau to stop being so silly and making such a fuss, and added with a certain amount of effrontery that the boy's possible fear of the physical pain involved was unfounded. Rousseau felt somewhat confused, decided that he had given the whole question far more importance than it deserved, and that was the end of it. Shortly thereafter he made his profession of faith and left the hospice. [23]

There is evidently an enormous amount of "fiction" in the earlier version of the episode. This same tendency to fictionalize (and romanticize) biographical material can be seen in *La Nouvelle Héloïse*, and in so far as the *Emile* as well is a novel (a *Bildungsroman*), this procedure is normal. What is disconcerting, however, is that Rousseau, in introducing this very episode, should choose to remark: "Lecteurs, ne craignez pas de moi des précautions indignes d'un ami de la vérité: je n'oublierai jamais ma devise [....] Je garantis la vérité des faits qui vont être rapportés, ils sont réellement arrivés à l'auteur du papier que je vais transcrire." Rousseau is performing here the same kind of dance (truth-or-fiction?) that we saw in the prefaces to *La Nouvelle Héloïse;* he is neither lying nor telling the exact truth. He is himself the author of the paper he is about to transcribe. But

---

[22] *Emile*, pp. 314-315.
[23] *O. C.* I, pp. 66-68.

he does not reveal himself as such, and indeed by implication he presents the paper as the writing of another. [24] The guarantee of the truthfulness of the account (why should the question enter his mind?) would seem to reveal an uneasy conscience, perhaps even a gnawing sense of bad faith in presenting an adulterated version of the truth.

The question necessarily arises concerning what kind of faith the reader may put in the numerous other supposedly "faithful accounts" that Rousseau presents in the *Emile* and elsewhere as empirical evidence supporting his theories. What about the story of the mother who gave her little boy the odd explanation of childbirth? What about the story of the spoiled child who took pleasure in waking Rousseau up during the middle of the night? Many of these accounts have been proven inaccurate by scholarly research. Clearly, the truthfulness of Rousseau's accounts is irrelevant to our understanding of his ideas, but a consideration of the distortion involved may lead nonetheless to some fruitful speculation on his own sense of his relationship to his reader. Significantly, one of Formey's criticisms had to do with the fact that Rousseau's procedures are always "marqués au coin de la singularité." [25] And, in fact, the "singular," romanesque element

---

[24] Rousseau was deeply concerned about the presentation of fiction as a document. His questioning, in the Quatrième Promenade, of Montesquieu's morality in presenting the *Temple de Gnide* as the translation of a Greek manuscript, a "history," reflects his own uneasiness over his semi-prevarications, or at least lack of candor, in his own presentation of *La Nouvelle Héloïse*. Similarly, in his defenses of the *Emile* he will frequently point out the "unfairness" of the authorities in condemning him *personally* for the ideas in the "Profession de foi" when, presumably, they had no way of knowing whether he or a real Savoyard vicar was in fact the author of that section of the *Emile*. This typical avoidance of guilt through accusation again covers a self-accusation: Rousseau, the bearer of truth, has lied! In any case, the strategy of self-justification is sheer sophistry: the strategist has nothing on his side but an empty shell of logic, and he knows it. No-one was taken in by the presentation of the "Profession" as the thoughts of another man. Formey picks up the formula "Je vous dirai ce que pensait un homme qui valait mieux que moi" and demolishes it with disgust: "Toujours des fictions. Pourquoi biaiser en pareil cas? M. R. n'a pas pu douter qu'on mettroit sur son compte tout ce qui se trouve dans son Livre? Il faloit donc l'avouer sans tergiversation" (*Anti-Emile*, Berlin, Pauli, 1763, p. 152).

[25] Formey, p. 202.

of this account of the Turin story is due precisely to Rousseau's misrepresentation of it, to his *untruth*. The author has no legitimate defense against Formey's criticisms if he himself is not scrupulously truthful: the slightest departure from truth dissolves the *pacte littéraire,* and the reader returns to his natural state of freedom, the freedom to criticize and to reject. If Rousseau fails now to convince his reader, if he fails to establish that blessed unity of vision, he has only himself to blame. Worse still, he can be considered guilty of fraud, and may be punished as a malefactor. This will be, for Rousseau, the haunting issue during the years following the publication of the *Emile:* is he guilty or innocent, should he or should he not be punished? Obsessed with the unjust condemnation and denunciation of what he *must* continue to consider his good doctrine and innocent person, he will spend most of the remainder of his career as a writer attempting to justify his writings by revealing his innocence as a human being. Clinging to his basic tenet that Rousseau's truth, scrupulously told, will finally convince the reader and draw him into communion with the writer, he has no choice but to plunge into what he calls at the beginning of the *Confessions* the "enterprise qui n'eut jamais d'exemple," the telling of the whole truth about himself. Only thus will he be able to purge himself of hidden doubts that he may not be worthy, or may not be considered worthy, of his motto. He, Jean-Jacques, is totally innocent. Rousseau must therefore be telling the truth.

It is understandable in any case that one obsessed with truth would sooner or later abandon his interpretation of the external world and of man in general in favor of the exploration and analysis of the inner world, the world of the self. Rousseau will admit, in his *Rêveries,* that this latter domain is not as easy to explore as he had thought in writing his *Confessions,* but it is nonetheless the most accessible area of all, providing the wondrously paradoxical (and profoundly illusory) assurance of subjectivity.

CHAPTER III

THE READER AS JUDGE

If Rousseau is now ready to "phase out" of his rôle as pur-veyor of public truth and to start presenting himself instead as the private figure Jean-Jacques, the transition is far from sudden. To be sure, he had insisted in all his works on introducing himself as a private figure, individualizing himself and providing himself with a face. In this he had an evident predecessor, Montaigne; but in the mid-18th Century the gesture is striking, so strong was the persistence of the Classical canon of impersonality. The public in turn responded by referring to Rousseau by his first name (he makes mention of the fashion already in the *Lettre à d'Alembert*). Formey even uses as the epigraph to his *Anti-Emile* a remark made to Rousseau by an unidentified lady and reported in the *Emile:* "Tais-toi, Jean-Jacques." Doubtless Formey felt fully justified in dealing so cavalierly with an author who signed his works and who spoke of his private life in print.

Jean Starobinski has dealt with the psychological roots and with certain literary manifestations of Rousseau's exhibitionism. Of interest for the present study is the manner in which his longing to reveal (or unveil) himself appears specifically in his relations with his reader.

Already during the period in which he was awaiting the publication of the *Emile* Rousseau was turning towards auto-biography. His publisher, Rey, suggested to him in December, 1761, that he write his memoirs. And in January, 1762, he wrote the four *Lettres à M. de Malesherbes,* his first important attempt at self-assessment and self-revelation. [1] The rhetorical situation of these letters is relatively simple. Rousseau is, for once, really directing his discourse to the person to whom the work is ostensibly addressed. He is, as it were, trying out his justifications on a single reader before taking on all of humanity. Yet we should not forget that Malesherbes, if a friend and protector of Rousseau's, was also the chief of the censorship bureau. Thus he represented public approval or disapproval; and, realistically, much seemed at the time to depend upon his "view" of Rousseau, even if in the long run not even his position proved sufficient to protect the beleaguered author from a peculiar combination of disadvantageous circumstances and hostile forces. In a sense, then, Rousseau presents his self-justification to a judge invested with the power of handing down a verdict.

✿   ✿   ✿

LETTRE A CRISTOPHE DE BEAUMONT (1763) and LETTRES ÉCRITES
DE LA MONTAGNE (1764)

The two great polemical letters, to the Archbishop of Paris and to the Genevan author of the *Lettres écrites de la campagne* (Jean-Robert Tronchin), are also addressed to men in the position of judge. It was by the decree issued from the archbishop's chancellery that the *Emile* was condemned and consigned to the flames, and it was through the power of the Genevan aristocrats, of whom Tronchin is the spokesman, that it had suffered a like fate in Rousseau's native republic.

Both of these letters are directed to clearly identifiable individuals. Yet in both Rousseau is addressing himself to the figure in question only as a pretext. He makes it clear from the outset that he has in fact nothing to say to the archbishop: "Pourquoi faut-il, Monseigneur, que j'aye quelque chose à vous dire? Quelle langue commune pouvons-nous parler, comment

---

[1] *Le Persifleur*, dating from 1749, is a conventional self-portrait, not a self-revelation of the kind that will account for the large part of Rousseau's literary enterprise after 1762.

pouvons-nous nous entendre, et qu'y a-t-il entre vous et moi?" [2]
The answer to the questions can easily be supplied, in a series of
negatives. Rousseau may address the archbishop endlessly in the
second person, but the work is in fact written for another set
of readers, just as Cicero's Catalinian Orations are addressed
to Catalina but directed at the Senate. Why would Rousseau
bother to summarize his public life for the benefit of the prelate,
as he does at the beginning of the letter? It is not to Beaumont
—who has already passed judgment— that he presents this jus-
tificatory glimpse of himself, but to the public that may have
been or may yet be influenced by the archbishop's "libels"
against Rousseau's person and doctrine. Typically Rousseau attempts to enlist the reader in his own ranks, creating a party
of the just. A passage near the end of the work reveals this
strategy clearly. Generalizing from Beaumont to *all* abusive power
and from himself to *all* of its victims, he carefully implicates the
reader in the latter group:

> Que vous discourez à votre aise, vous autres hommes
> constitués en dignité! [...] Sur les moindres convenances
> d'intérêt ou d'état, vous nous balayez devant vous com-
> me la poussière [...] Quand vous nous insultez impuné-
> ment, il ne nous est même pas permis de nous plaindre,
> et si nous montrons notre innocence et vos torts, on nous
> accuse encore de vous manquer de respect. [3]

Rousseau's fundamental posture, as an advocate in his own defense
appearing before the bench in the presence of the accuser, takes
explicit form in the final paragraph of the work:

> Si vous étiez un particulier comme moi, que je puisse
> vous citer devant un Tribunal équitable, et que nous
> comparussions tous deux, moi avec mon Livre, et
> vous avec votre Mandement; vous y seriez certainement
> déclaré coupable, et condamné à me faire une réparation
> aussi publique que l'offense l'a été. [4]

Rousseau could have found no better description of the procedure
he has followed in this work: a comparison of the two writings

[2] Ed. cit., p. 5.
[3] Ibid., pp. 194-195.
[4] Ibid., pp. 195-196.

in front of the jury of readers. Both this procedure and the strategy of dissociating the reader from the archbishop (through ridicule of the latter) converge near the end of the letter in a passage reminiscent of the *Réponse à une lettre anonyme*. Rousseau transcribes a passage from the decree describing the Genevan's career, works, and character, using once again the technique of refutational asides:

> *Du sein de l'erreur* (il est vrai que j'ai passé ma jeunesse dans votre église) *il s'est élevé* (pas fort haut) *un homme plein du langage de la philosophie,* (comment prendrois-je un langage que je n'entends point?) *sans être véritablement philosophe:* (Oh! d'accord: je n'aspirai jamais à ce titre, auquel je reconnais n'avoir aucun droit; et je n'y renonce assurément pas par modestie.) [etc.] [5]

Rousseau liked to claim that he never indulged in personal satire, yet here he is systematically deflating Beaumont thorough satirical asides the technique of which is drawn from comedy. As one character speaks, the other comments on his lines to the audience. What is essential to the comic effect of this type of scene is precisely that the audience, hearing the satirical commentary, forms a complicity of ridicule with the satirist. The audience becomes an approving witness to the deflation, and as such is requisite to the satirical strategy.

So far, the self-justification seems quite simple. Rousseau counts on his reader's willingness to enter into complicity with him. Unfortunately, the *Lettre à Christophe de Beaumont* could have no effect whatsoever on the actual course of events. Written after the fact, it was merely an easy gesture in deference to convention: one is persecuted, one defends oneself.

In the *Lettres écrites de la montagne*, Rousseau has already moved beyond the easy self-justification of the previous letter. Here, the obsession with guilt, and the conviction that a *personal* justification alone can provide revindication for the written doctrine, come to the surface. The issues are clearly set up in the Première Lettre, which reveals the state of mind of the author

---

[5] Ibid., p. 189.

just prior to the commencement of work on the *Confessions*. First, on the question of guilt:

> Je suis homme et j'ai fait des Livres; j'ai donc fait aussi des erreurs. [A footnote to this statement excepts geometricians from this generalization, but then casts doubt even on the absolute truth of geometry: "La science a beau être infaillible; l'homme qui la cultive se trompe souvent.] [...] Mais quel Auteur n'est pas dans le même cas, ou s'ose flatter de n'y pas être? Là-dessus donc, point de dispute. Si l'on me réfute et qu'on ait raison, l'erreur est corrigée et je me tais. Si l'on me réfute et qu'on ait tort, je me tais encore; dois-je répondre du fait d'autrui? En tout état de cause, après avoir entendu les deux Parties, le public est juge, il prononce, le livre triomphe ou tombe, et le procès est fini. [6]

Rousseau still sees himself before the bench, wrestling with the issues of right and wrong, which the Public will finally determine. But is the Public's judgement completely reliable? Rousseau seems to harbor doubts on the subject, doubts founded on the principle of universal opacity and fallibility. A surer criterion of innocence, one that resides in *intention*, must be found:

> Un homme n'est pas coupable pour nuire en voulant servir, et si l'on poursuivoit criminellement un Auteur pour des fautes d'ignorance ou d'inadvertance, pour de mauvises maximes qu'on pourroit tirer de ses écrits très conséquemment mais contre son gré, quel Ecrivain pourroit se mettre à l'abri? Il faudroit être inspiré du Saint Esprit pour se faire Auteur et n'avoir que des gens inspirés du Saint Esprit pour juges. [7]

Rousseau held consistently to this morality of intention, which was doubtless attractive to him precisely because it gives the subject absolute assurance of his guilt or innocence. He may thus dispense with the external judgement. The perfect image of the state of self-containment towards which Rousseau aspires is precisely that of the Holy Spirit, perfect wisdom and justice,

---

[6] *O. C.* III, p. 691.
[7] Ibid., p. 692.

reflecting upon itself. So far, however, he is not willing to abandon at least the possibility of a reflection from outside, an "objective" judgment. He is, he admits, not an angel, and therefore
is capable of making mistakes; but:

> ces fautes qu'on prétend trouver dans mes Ecrits peuvent
> fort bien n'y pas être, parce que ceux qui les y trou-
> vent ne sont pas des Anges, non plus. Hommes et sujets
> à l'erreur ainsi que moi, sur quoi prétendent-ils que leur
> raison soit l'arbitre de la mienne, et que je sois punissable
> pour n'avoir pas pensé comme eux?
>   Le public est donc le juge de semblables fautes; son
> blâme en est le seul châtiment. Nul ne peut se soustraire
> à ce Juge, et quant-à-moi je n'en apelle pas. [8]

Magically, the Public, although made up of men, is not subject
to the errors in judgment that plague Beaumont and Tronchin and
all the other persecutors. Rousseau makes an act of faith: the
Public occupies (as the choice of expression —"nul ne peut se
soustraire à ce juge"— indicates) the privileged position of the
Holy Spirit, all-knowing and all-just. And just as the reader of
the *Emile* was to have magical powers of intuition, so the public
will know the author's intention intuitively. Prerequisite to guilt,
evil intention can be discerned in the very way in which the
book is written, in the manner of argument. "Si cette intention
est évidemment mauvaise, ce n'est plus erreur, ni faute, c'est
crime; ici tout change." [9] The public, then, "feels" the author's
guilt or innocence in the very presentation, just as the ideal reader
of the *Emile* was to "feel" that the mountebank's discourse had
been dictated by the Tutor. Rousseau has recreated the ideal
reader, this time not as pupil but as judge.

The plea will then become a matter of *style*. The way Rousseau writes and the way he lives (i. e., his literary and existential
styles) will become the prime exhibits in persuading the public
of the innocence of his intentions. A man who lives and writes
as he does cannot be a public poisoner, he will repeat time and
again. It is worth noting in this connection that Rousseau's

---

[8] Idem.
[9] Ibid., p. 693.

primary consideration in the foreword to the *Lettres écrites de la montagne* bears on the question of style:

> Qu'on ne cherche pas même ici dans le style le dédommagement de l'aridité de la matière. Ceux que quelques traits heureux de ma plume ont si fort irrités trouveront de quoi s'apaiser dans ces Lettres [...] J'aurai donc trouvé grace en ce point devant ceux qui s'imaginent qu'il est essenciel à la vérité d'être dite froidement; opinion que pourtant j'ai peine à comprendre. Lorsqu'une vive persuasion nous anime, le moyen d'employer un langage glacé? Quand Archimede tout transporté couroit nud dans les rues de Syracuse, en avoit-il moins trouvé la vérité parce qu'il se passionnoit pour elle? Tout au contraire, celui qui la sent ne peut s'abstenir de l'adorer; celui qui demeure froid ne l'a pas vue.
>
> Quoi qu'il en soit, je prie les Lecteurs de vouloir bien mettre à part mon beau style, et d'examiner seulement si je raisonne bien ou mal; car enfin, de cela seul qu'un Auteur s'exprime en bons termes, je ne vois pas comment il peut s'ensuivre que cet Auteur ne sait ce qu'il dit. [10]

All this is in answer to the charges of "éloquence funeste" launched against him by his enemies. In view of Rousseau's ambivalent feelings about embroidery of the truth, the problem of style as possible distortion or defiguration must have bothered him greatly. He will later make a careful distinction at the beginning of the *Dialogues* between *force* and *faste* as attributes of style, affirming that if Jean-Jacques' style possesses the latter quality rather than the former, then he is indeed the person that his enemies have made him out to be. And he will claim in his *Confessions* not to care very much for his First Discourse because of its rather ornate rhetoric. We can, indeed, see a clear progression in his career from the traditional rhetoric of the First Discourse to the pure "song of the self," the individualized language of the *Rêveries*. The problem confronting Rousseau at the time of the remarks quoted above was: how to avoid the evident forms of persuasive rhetoric (regarded as "traits heureux") that might be considered seductive and therefore "ill-intentioned," while still retaining the warmth and passion that alone bespeak

---

10 Ibid., pp. 685-686.

the truth. The image of Archimedes running naked through the streets is doubly appropriate. Rousseau is about to start appearing naked as well, in his *Confessions,* and he will see this action as a revelation of truth. In addition, nudity signifies not only truth but lack of adornment. The *bare* truth is alone exact and trustworthy. The style of the *Confessions,* while recognizably of its time, is in fact remarkably free of the conventional rhetoric taught in the schools. Moreover, it shows in its sentence structure far less influence of the Latin models (with their emphasis on cadence, period, and balance) than do the earlier works. Historically a milestone in the development of modern French prose style, the *Confessions* reflect in Rousseau's own stylistic evolution the need for a medium capable of conveying the warmth and passion of personal conviction while dispensing with the suspect —because conventional— attributes of persuasive writing.

＊　＊　＊

THE "CONFESSIONS" (1765-1770)

Having chosen the public as his judge, Rousseau need only present his case. He appears before the public tribunal in the *Confessions* and the *Dialogues, ou Rousseau juge de Jean-Jacques.*

In the *Confessions,* the reader represents the public, but the public seen in a particular light. Rousseau distinguishes at this point between his "enemies," guilty of attempting to present the innocent Jean-Jacques as a monster, and the public, as yet only waiting to choose between Rousseau's true Jean-Jacques and the false Jean-Jacques fabricated by his enemies. The writer's task is to make the reader see him as he sees himself. As a corollary, the success of this task will induce a recognition of his goodness and innocence. And, as a final step, the reader is to undergo a moral reformation by adopting Rousseau, whose goodness he has recognized, as a model. The reader, then, is following Rousseau, always one step behind. The relationship with the reader is thus quite peaceful and friendly. There are few anticipated objections; there are, in fact, relatively few direct references to the reader, and most of these are in the third person rather than the second (as if the reader were not within the screen of vision). [11] The tale-teller, lost in his tale, is surrounded by a group of children hanging on every word. He appears to be split in two, pointing to himself as the hero of the tale, frequently using the locutions "me voici" and "me voilà." The gesture of pointing is made for the benefit of the witness, who is meant to share the feelings both of Jean-Jacques the agent and Rousseau the narrator (they nearly always coincide, except in the rare instances where the agent has to appear ridiculous). "O vous, lecteurs curieux de la grande histoire du noyer de la terrasse, écoutez-en l'horrible tragédie, et vous abstenez de frémir, si vous pouvez"; "Lecteur pitoyable, partagez mon affliction." [12] He assumes on his own part an enormous influence on his reader: "Si je disois mes raisons [i. e., for the abandonment of his children], j'en dirois trop. Puisqu'elles ont pu me séduire elles en séduiroient bien d'autres: je ne veux pas exposer les jeunes gens qui pourroient me lire à se laisser abuser par la même erreur." [13] He sees the reader following his every step, "learning" Rousseau: "Que fis-je en cette occasion? Déjà mon Lecteur l'a deviné, pour peu qu'il m'ait suivi jusqu'ici." [14]

As in the *Emile*, however, the real reader does not necessarily accept the role Rousseau assigns to him. He may believe only

---

[11] For a suggestive discussion of Rousseau's "dialogue" with the reader in this work, see Jacques Voisine, "Le dialogue avec le lecteur dans *Les Confessions*," *Jean-Jacques Rousseau et son œuvre. Actes et colloques, 2* (ed. J. Fabre), Paris (Klincksieck), 1964, pp. 23-31. M. Voisine points out the perspective of "singularity" in which Rousseau sees himself, and which becomes one of the recurrent motifs of his dialogue with the reader. The writer is describing the only man left uncorrupted by convention, whose motives, reactions, and reflections are therefore hard for the reader to understand. Frequently his comments to the reader have the purpose of retraining the reader to sees things as Rousseau, the natural man, does. In this sense, the dialogue with the reader reflects the general aim of the work as I understand it. I would mildly disagree with M. Voisine only regarding his insistence on the gradual transformation of the reader into an enemy. There are, to be sure, a few passages in the *Confessions* (especially towards the end) where the reader does appear to join the camp of the "enemies" who willfully and maliciously misunderstand Rousseau, but in the vast majority of instances the reader appears as a docile follower in Rousseau's footsteps, as a willing trainee.

[12] *O. C.* I, pp. 22, 39.

[13] Ibid., p. 357.

[14] Ibid., p. 427.

part of what he reads, he may not feel Rousseau's own feelings, or he may not feel them with the proper intensity. He is a free agent. But it is typical of Rousseau not to be able to understand the relative nature of freedom and obligation. Both existed for him as absolutes. (When he feels *obliged* to give the little boy alms —as he tells us in the Sixième Promenade— he automatically asserts his absolute freedom by changing the route of his daily walk; failing to see that his freedom is a form of servitude.) For Rousseau, the reader either reads him or not, but if he does he *must* honor the terms of the pact and become Rousseau's reader. This explains why Rousseau so frequently affiirms his unwillingness to be read by those incapable of reading him "properly." He conceives of the reader who does not subscribe fully to the contract as a hypocrite and an evil person.

If he wishes to avoid "becoming" Rousseau, the reader finds himself obliged to step back, to remove himself from the work. He must read with an uncomfortable "double focus," Rousseau's and his own. Nothing could be more instructive in this regard than a consideration of the final section of Book IX, in which Rousseau recounts the events leading up to his precipitous departure from L'Hermitage. Reading this account for the first time, without benefit of notes or prior information, we are bound to feel oddly disconcerted. On the one hand, we are swept along with Rousseau (whom we have no reason to mistrust) on a wave of righteous indignation. On the other hand, it is at the very least difficult to conceive what Rousseau found so thoroughly offensive in the various letters he received from Diderot, Grimm, and Mme d'Epinay. Out of this contradiction there grows (as I remember from my own first reading of the work) a feeling of confusion that makes the events seem somehow unreal. The impression is not unlike that produced by the opening pages of Kafka's *Metamorphosis* in which the thread of inconsequential discourse running through Gregor Samsa's mind seems inappropriate to the horrendous situation in which he finds himself. In Rousseau's case, naturally, the converse is true: one has the impression of a dream in which powerful emotions are unleashed by rationally inconsequential events. Here, all that seems real is the feeling. The letters that Rousseau transcribes appear almost as blank spots or mumblings between the eloquent passages of

emotional reaction, and there seems to be practically no relationship between the two elements of the account. One finishes
reading Diderot's slightly presumptuous or Grimm's somewhat
oblique letter only to plunge into such locutions as: "Le trem-
blement de colère, l'éblouissement qui me gagnoient en lisant ce
billet [...]". "Quand le premier transport de mon indignation me
permit d'écrire [...]"; "Frappé d'étonnement en lisant cette lettre,
je cherchois avec inquiétude ce qu'elle pouvoit signifier [...]."
The reader goes back over the letters in vain, he cannot find
in them the motive for Rousseau's outrage. The author appears to
have the reader up against the wall: he must either believe
in and identify himself with the author (and not just with a clinical
understanding of the irrational motives for his reactions) or he
must stand outside the work and refuse to "be" Rousseau.
If he makes the first option, he must assume that the letters are in
some mysterious way insulting (perhaps the reader is less perceptive than Rousseau), and then "feel" with Rousseau in much
the same way a small child "feels" with its mother: the emotion
is communicated even if the stimulus is unseen or uncomprehended.
This option, for solidarity, is in a sense the easy one to make.
Rousseau is, after all, not presenting the account as a dream or
a fantasy, quite the contrary. He does not begin, as Kafka does,
with an obvious fiction. And since we are accustomed to accept
the validity of what is placed before us until we have clear
reason not to, we tend to side with Rousseau and share his
feelings. Besides, it is quite simply more exciting, more pleasu-
rable, to share Rousseau's emotion. The author gives us the
opportunity to relive with him an intensely dramatic (even tragic,
in its presentation) episode in which we, the noble and the just,
will find ourselves hounded out into the snow, like King Lear
into the storm. Why resist?

The second option is easy to make if we possess the knowledge
that Rousseau takes pains to suppress (for example, the actual
—and not very admirable— contents of the "lettre aussi honnête
qu'elle pouvoit l'être" that he tells us he sent to Mme d'Epinay),
and that scholars have placed at our disposal. The option for
"disengagement" is easy to make if we have the sophistication in
Rousseauism provided by Babbitt, Raymond, Osmont, Guéhenno,
Starobinski, Eigeldinger, and many others now. If we read the

episode "objectively," we see Rousseau, or make an effort to see him, through the eyes of Grimm, Diderot, and Mme d'Epinay. We perhaps admire the forthrightness, dignity, and perception displayed by Mme d'Epinay in her final letter. We may surmise that Grimm was attempting to give Rousseau good, practical advice without compromising his position with Mme d'Epinay. We finally *understand* the letters, but at Rousseau's expense. We are not the reader Rousseau wants, the reader who is at one with him. We are to make the first option, and see Rousseau not through the eyes of others, but through his own eyes. We are to inhabit him and be imprisoned by him as he was by himself.

The question of the reader's option is fraught with complicating factors. First of all, as Starobinski has suggested, [15] it may well be not the particular option made that lies at the heart of the matter but rather the very fact of the reader's being placed in the position of having to choose *absolutely* between Rousseau and his "enemies." Either choice will do, as long as it is clear and absolute. The basis of the contract Rousseau has established with his reader appears in the Eighth Book: "C'est à moi d'être vrai, c'est au lecteur d'être juste." [16] Rousseau is writing for the purpose of obtaining a verdict. If he loses, he will simply take his case to a higher tribunal than that of the public. After all, in the opening pages of the *Confessions* he sees himself presenting his book not only to the court of mankind (all men who ever have existed or ever will exist) but to God as well. His thirst for judgment appears clearly in the circumstances of his private readings of the Second Part of the *Confessions* in Paris. He terminated one of his readings (early in May, 1771) with the following words:

> J'ai dit la vérité. Si quelqu'un sait des choses contraires à ce que je viens d'exposer, fussent-elles mille fois prouvées, il sait des mensonges et des impostures, et s'il refuse de les approfondir et de les eclaircir avec moi tandis que je suis en vie il n'aime ni la justice ni la vérité. Pour moi je le déclare hautement et sans crainte: Quiconque, même sans avoir lu mes écrits, examinera par ses propres yeux mon naturel, mon caractère, mes moeurs, mes

---

[15] Op. cit., pp. 312-315.
[16] *O. C.* I, p. 359.

> penchans, mes plaisirs, mes habitudes et pourra me croire un malhonnête homme, est lui-même un homme à étouffer. [17]

He added later, as a commentary on the listeners' reaction to his reading:

> J'achevai ainsi ma lecture et tout le monde se tut. Mad^e Egmont fut la seule qui me parut émue; elle tressaillit visiblement; mais elle se remit bien vite, et garda le silence ainsi que toute la compagnie. Tel fut le fruit que je tirai de cette lecture et de ma déclaration.

Rousseau's disappointment is understandable. According to the convention regulating the writing of the *Confessions* he is supposed to have received his "fruit," a verdict. And, indeed, in the contemporary account of another of Rousseau's readings of the *Confessions,* he is represented as having paused after the account of the abandonment of his children, "attendant une objection, la souhaitant même,"; [18] but no one spoke up, and after dinner he returned to the subject, defending himself eloquently (as if he had in fact been judged guilty). What was unbearable was the silence, the absence of a verdict.

The infrequency in the *Confessions* of overt attempts to influence the reader's judgment would seem to lend support to the hypothesis that the reader is meant to judge impartially but absolutely. Even in the famous account of the theft of the ribbon Rousseau's self-justification seems to be directed towards himself and his own conscience rather than towards the reader; he seems in fact to be talking to himself. Still, it would be idle to maintain that the author cares not at all about the kind of judgment the reader will hand down. As we have seen, he takes pains to present himself in a favorable light. If nothing is ever his fault, how can we consider him guilty? We must, then, return to the question of the two options.

It would seem as if we are obliged, in making our choice, to err in one way or another. In a sense, we may be reading the *Confessions* unfairly if we refuse to do what, esthetically and

---

[17] Ibid., p. 656.
[18] Ibid., p. 1613.

psychologically, the author appears to be asking us to do (i.e., to identify ourselves entirely with him, to enter into his skin, and to see him exclusively through his own eyes). Perhaps the Romantics were more faithful in their reading of the *Confessions* than we are nowadays, even if they may have *understood* Rousseau, in all his complexity, far less accurately than we do. The rhetorical postulate of such a work (and of most non-ironic Romantic writing) is that the reader is asked to step into the work where he will be reborn according to the model given him. Rousseau's dream is a world of creatures fashioned in his own image, a Clarens. It seems to be a good deal to ask of reader, in terms of self-abnegation, but it may well be that in refusing to comply we are misreading the work. Does this mean, then, that we can no longer read the *Confessions* properly? Must we read it, at best, with kindly, somewhat superior sympathy, or with clinical acumen? Is it fair to refuse to follow Rousseau out into the snow when we willingly follow Lear out into the rain? These questions invoke issues that go far beyond merely our reading of the *Confessions*. They invite us to consider the nature of the author-reader relationship in romantic literature in general.[19]

We may distinguish between two radically different modes of literary presentation, neither of which perhaps has ever existed in a "pure" state, but which it is useful to isolate for purposes of discussion. One is, for want of an established term, direct. The work is presented to the reader without intermediary. It is of course the product of the writer's way of seeing things and of the multiple expressive choices he has made. But the mode of vision and the storehouse of expressions are conceived by the writer as being public, shared. Hence, he *feels* (and this feeling is all-important in terms of the manner in which he will conceive of his relationship to the reader) as if he is providing his reader

---

[19] By "romantic" I do not mean to designate merely the Romantic School of even the Romantic movement. I am following Irving Babbitt and, more recently, René Girard in their use of the term to designate a particular kind of character, vision, and sense of relationship. I am particularly indebted to Professor Girard (*Mensonge romantique et vérité romanesque,* Paris, 1961) for his notion of the triangular relationship between subject and object through model, which I find thoroughly relevant to the writer-reader relationship in Rousseau's works.

primarily with an object, not with a pair of glasses. The author is a mirror rather than a lens. This mode of thought seems to have been predominant, to greater or lesser degree, before the development in modern times of the identity-dissimilarity obsession analyzed by Professor Girard. [20] It would seem that for the pre-modern writer, literary creation did not involve a process of seduction to the writer's own point of view so much as an incorporation into the literary object, by use of a vast reservoir of conventions, of a "right" perception of the object, the "rightness" of which was conceived basically not in subjective but in objective terms. Dante's representation of himself as a *scribe* throughout the *Commedia* exemplifies this mode to perfection. The underlying assumption in this tradition is the existence of a community, an agreement; hence the easy and prevalent use of convention and the relative unimportance of what we would call "personal" or "subjective" literature.

The other radical mode of literary presentation is, again for want of an established term, mediated. Here, the writer's task consists not merely in placing his creation before the reader, but (more urgently) in taking steps to insure an identity of vision and feeling between the reader and himself. The writer does not intend to have the reader perceive a public object but rather a private object as seen through the eyes of the subject. Implicit in this preoccupation with identity of vision and feeling (giving rise to an attempt at seduction) is the assumption of an undesirable and threatening difference between writer and reader. The romantic writer thus becomes involved in an enterprise of self-aggrandisement; he presents *himself*, basically, as a model (whether directly through self-revelation or indirectly through the forceful imposition of *his* way of seeing and feeling), and the success of his enterprise can be measured in terms of how many Werthers, how many Renés, how many Jean-Jacques are born of his effort. In the last analysis, Rousseau wished to spawn as many Rousseaus as there would be readers of the *Confessions* (or of his other works, for that matter). They would be his perfect progeny. He

---

[20] Op. cit. By "modern times" I do not mean to designate anything more specific than post-medieval. It is evident that cultural developments such as this take place slowly and fitfully.

had abandoned his real children because he could not bear to see them grow up under any influence other than his (their grandmother would surely turn them into monsters, i.e., something different from himself). Through the magic of his book he attempts to work the miracle denied him in the real world. Small wonder that nowadays many of us should read this kind of literature either with a mixture of fascination and loathing, with self-protective irony, or, in the case of most modern scholars, with equally self-protective intellectual detachment.

Returning now to the question of what constitutes a "valid" reading of the *Confessions:* can we find no way of reading Rousseau's masterpiece without becoming Rousseau, without entering the prison he has prepared for us? Or should we, perhaps, as good readers, submit to the imprisonment temporarily? As the product of a genius who carried every principle to its ultimate consequences, the *Confessions* should provide as good a set of materials for a general study of the problems involved as we could possibly find.

Certain points of relevance must be established. Since the announced purpose of the *Confessions* is apologetic, and since self-justification doubtless had much to do with Rousseau's original impulse to write the work, we cannot help considering it in terms of its success as an apology. Rousseau's objectivity and veracity become legitimate issues for the reader, who has been "dared" (as we see in the final page of the work) to judge the author guilty. The reader is naturally curious to know whether or not he is, indeed, an "homme à étouffer." The author asserts his own moral integrity, and places the moral integrity of the reader on trial: it is natural to respond to this challenge by attempting to bring the author down to a lower level than the one he has assumed, and to deal with his threat by convicting him of dishonesty. [21] In approaching the unmediated work, we see the

---

[21] One of the supreme ironies of romantic literature is precisely the inevitable temptation to "push back" that the writer's aggression inspires in the reader. With what would seem to be a genius for failure, the romantic writer frequently achieves the contrary of what he has set out to do, and the reader not only fails to take the writer as his model but consciously rejects him as such. Perhaps the writer has, however, achieved a more important aim: he has provoked the reader into an identity duel in which there *can be* a winner and a loser.

things that the author saw, and from his moral perspective. We see Lear and Goneril, moreover, not only as they are but in their entirety. There is no question of reading the letters and memoirs of Goneril, because they do not exist. The "truth" about Goneril or Lear and the truth about Rousseau are thus different orders of truth. In one case, all the evidence is available. In the other, we are confronted with a romantic mediation; the order of truth changes, and with it the principles of judgement. We are justified in seeking to complement Rousseau's account with Mme d'Epinay's, just as Mme d'Epinay was justified in seeking an injunction against Rousseau's readings of material that she considered slanderous. For her, the work was not "just" a work of art.

The reader's role does, then, consist partially in entering into the game that Rousseau has set up. The reading is no longer merely a distanced (esthetic) experience, but becomes an encounter in which our actual judgement of the author as a man, and our judgement of ourselves in relation to him, are brought into play. In this sense, when the reader passes a moral judgement on Rousseau, perhaps finding him guilty of dishonesty, he is merely doing what the work asks him to do.

The reader is being asked, as we have suggested, to involve his own identity in his reading. The reading implies a comparison of value (essential to the sado-masochistic syndrome), in which the reader is invited to measure himself against the writer, the model. Rousseau signals this aspect of the reader's role in the Judgment Day scene at the beginning of the work. Jean-Jacques will bare himself, revealing the model, after which each man will in turn examine himself in comparison with the model offered. This aspect of the work appears even more clearly in the "Ebauche des *Confessions*" (1764). Rousseau develops there at considerable length the notion of the usefulness of his self-revelation for men, whom he will provide with a means of defining themselves (self-definition being possible only through comparison with the other). In the *Confessions*, he abandons this altruistic rationalization, hurling a challenge instead: "Que chacun d'eux découvre à son tour son cœur aux pieds de ton trône avec la même sincérité; et puis qu'un seul te dise, s'il l'ose: je fus meilleur que cet homme-là." [22] Rousseau is interested in subjugating the reader, in having the reader recognize his own inferiority to the model offered (which, of course, paves the way for imitation of the model).

To this extent, then, the *Confessions* and all mediated works are not merely objects but *gestures,* and the reader responds appropriately with a gesture. The gesture is part of the esthetic of the work, if we are willing to admit in the definition of the term an element violating the requirement of psychic distance. The author of the mediated work, moreover, takes the risk of his gesture: he will be judged along with his work. It is part of the covenant of his writing. The "unsophisticated" reader who frankly admits his hatred, love, contempt, envy of Rousseau or Chateaubriand (or Voltaire, for that matter, since his works are highly mediated) is a better reader than the one who would regard their works uniquely as esthetic objects. Georges Poulet considers Mme de Staël's reaction to Rousseau as typical of modern criticism, in that she takes as the point of departure her *admiration for the man,* which she wishes to express and which no one seems (to her) to have expressed before. [23] One might add that whether or not she is reacting in a specifically modern way she is clearly reading Rousseau as he wished to be read. She is judging *him,* and responding to *him,* through his work.

With this stated, however, we must recognize a dimension of the *Confessions* that remains sealed off from the writer's struggle to control and appropriate the reader. In large measure the work is a vision, a conception, and the reader can to that extent peer into it directly. The *je* through which the fiction is presented is not merely a voice of self-justification, but is also the familiar *je* of the first-person singular narrative. The use of the *je* does not necessarily betoken mediation between reader and object. It can serve as well (as it does in much 18th-century fiction) as a convenient entranceway into the author's world, thus permitting the identification typical of our relationship to characters perceived directly in relatively unmediated works of art. Psychic distance is maintained without sacrifice of the vicarious experience of the

---

[22] *O. C.* I, p. 5.
[23] Public lecture, Geneva, May 1966.

character's particular vision and feeling. In so far as the reader can safely listen to the *je* of the *Confessions* and translate this *je* into *moi* (as he does in reading, for example, *Gil Blas*), he can bring to the work the same principles of perception and judgment that he brings to *King Lear*. In other words, he can to this extent safely follow Rousseau out into the snow.

It is worth noting that the reader frequently enjoys this distanced identification in spite of the author. As usual, things are far more ambiguous than Rousseau would have them be: we are capable of standing within and outside of a character at one and the same time (or perhaps alternately, but with such rapidity that the effect is one of simultaneity). Thus we can identify ourselves with Rousseau the writer, bending to his seduction or refusing to do so, and identify ourselves in a different way with Rousseau the agent, the fiction. An appropriate reading of the work is based on a recognition of the double nature of Rousseau's enterprise. On one level, he wished to convince the reader of Rousseau's superiority. On another level, he wanted the reader to perceive and "feel" with the character Jean-Jacques whom Rousseau lovingly creates. Our vision of Jean-Jacques may not coincide with Rousseau's own conscious intention, and he would doubtless not understand our tolerance of this fact. But we see him as he desired to portray himself on a deeper level of truth than that of mere self-justification. He may suppress information, he may alter a host of minor circumstances in the account of his life: we nonetheless see him as he is, just as surely and as completely as we see Lear. What we perceive is the Jean-Jacques whom Rousseau knew intuitively, in a way far too complex for analytic description to convey, and in a perspective that transcends self-justification. We know him as Shakespeare knows Falstaff or Balzac Vautrin, i.e., as an idea given esthetic embodiment. In the instance, this idea is the self. And Rousseau, paradoxically, allows us to see this self as he himself never could: we see him in his "intolerable" ambiguity, through a massive accumulation of circumstances each of which adds a stroke to the portrait. Vile and noble, obtuse and profound, cowardly and courageous, painfully honest and deeply deceptive, he exists as an amalgam of attributes that gradually endow him in our eyes with the *definition* that he so craved. He becomes for us a figure, the Jean-Jacques of Rousseau.

In recreating himself as a figure, Rousseau achieves a paradoxical triumph. In order to avoid being seen as the object that his "enemies" would make him out to be, he has been forced to turn himself into an object. The object that he creates, however, is at least his *own*. His identity is safe from appropriation by the Other. Let future generations read Grimm, Diderot, Mme d'Epinay. Rousseau's self-portrait will henceforth exist not only as a refutation of their version of him, but still better as a memorial to the Self eternally immutable, indeed incapable hereafter of change. The *Confessions* proclaim: I am *my* self.

A similar defensive assertion of identity is perhaps at the root of all romantic autobiography. In Rousseau's case, protection of his identity surely constituted a major motivation in his writing, and a recognition of this motivation may lead to a deeper understanding of his conception of the reader as witness. Mankind is gathered before the author not merely to pass judgment on him, but also to perceive and acknowledge his identity as he himself understands it. The curiously ambiguous relationship thus established between writer and reader is signified in Rousseau's fantasy of appearing on Judgment Day *with his book in hand* to challenge humanity to a moral duel. It is not clear which object humanity is to observe, the man or the book. For Rousseau, they seem to be coterminal, yet if such were the case, either he or the book would be superfluous in the Judgment Day situation. But he prefers the triangular situation, in which the object Jean-Jacques will be perceived by the spectator through the eyes of Rousseau. Only thus can Rousseau the man be sure of being judged on the basis of his own recreation of himself. If he is present along with his book, it is only to remind the reader that a human being has stood as model for the statue, and the reader is not only to apprehend the statue but to judge, through it, the goodness of the model.

The situation in which the reader finds himself placed would normally be intolerable: he is expected to play simultaneously the double role of witness and judge. Rousseau manages, however, to solve this problem with impeccable logic. The reader's assent to the "thusness" of the object "Jean-Jacques" implies a favorable judgment as an automatic consequence. For to see Jean-Jacques possessing innocence as an essential attribute is to pronounce him innocent. Or, rather, there is no need even to pronounce, since the judgment is already implicit in the recognition.

As is so frequently the case, however, Rousseau's ingenious solution in the realm of logic does not work to perfection in reality. The reader is content to remain witness; the step to judgment, being automatic, requires no participation on the reader's part and therefore passes unnoticed. The plain fact is that the reader of the *Confessions* fails to cast himself as fully in the role of judge as the work seems by its logic to require him to do. The author has assured himself of an automatic judgment, out of the need to preserve his conviction of his innocence from corrosion: the reader *might* judge otherwise if left free. But guilt and innocence do not appear as burning issues when the defendant so easily resolves them for himself. The reader is, in fact, never given the hard task of forming a judgment: the judgment is both preliminary and automatic. Here as before Rousseau has set up an ideal, ever-assenting automaton of a reader. The real reader is still independent. As we have seen, Rousseau was bitterly disappointed by the reaction of his auditors in 1771. Yet these human beings had, for attending his readings, their own motives, none of which corresponded exactly to the motive attributed to them by the author. [24] Rousseau's Judgment Day was for them an entertainment. There was no doubt something unfair in the advantage the auditors took of Rousseau's compulsive self-revelation. According to one of them, they were aware of his mania, and if they listened attentively to his self-justifications, it was "pour avoir le plaisir d'en parler." [25] But Rousseau was as usual largely at fault for entering into a unilateral compact. The reader's reaction parallels that of Rousseau's auditors. The reader is perhaps kinder, but he too is there not to judge but to "have the pleasure" of seeing Rousseau. That he should neglect judgment as irrelevant is not his fault but the author's. Thus the author-reader relationship established for the purpose of self-justification proves to be as unsatisfactory

---

[24] *O. C.* I, pp. 1611-1614.
[25] Ibid., p. 1613.

as the relationship previously established for the propagation of the truth, and for much the same reason. Rousseau is still unable to transform the real reader into his ideal reader, or, in other words, to make himself understood as he wished to be (on a conscious level). His next literary enterprise will be a pure fantasy of wish-fulfillment in which he will once more "solve" the problem, as before with *La Nouvelle Héloïse,* by adopting a form that precludes the possibility of an author-reader relationship in the normal sense of the term, while giving free rein to Rousseau in his pursuit of the relationship according to his heart.

❉ ❉ ❉

DIALOGUES, OU ROUSSEAU JUGE DE JEAN-JACQUES (1772-1776)

The *Dialogues* consist of three conversations between Rousseau and a Frenchman, who discuss what the author sees by this time as "le cas Jean-Jacques": who is Jean-Jacques *really,* independently of the calumnies and misunderstandings of the public? Rousseau clearly considers the battle of the *Confessions* as lost; he has failed to make the public see him as he is. The only fruit of his work has been silence. But is it time yet to capitulate? Not so long as there remains the slightest chance of reshaping his reader. And so for four years Rousseau works laboriously, painfully, at this masterpiece of logic wrenched from its moorings in reality, in a last frantic effort to prove his innocence. Touchingly, he returns in his choice of epigraph to the very quotation from Ovid under which he had presented his first public work, the *Discours sur les sciences et les arts:* "Barbarus hic ego sum quia non intelligor illis." Over twenty years have passed, during which he has done everything in his power to make himself and his truth understood, yet Jean-Jacques remains the unintelligible outsider. Still, the choice of an epigraph that had heralded the triumphal appearance of a work destined to acquire him sudden *recognition* seems to betray a survival of his desire —perhaps even intent— to be seen, heard, and recognized in his truth. Once more, however, the attempt will prove abortive, for it will take place in the closed-off world of his own self-indulgent fantasy.

In the *Confessions,* Rousseau the author and Jean-Jacques the figure exist in illusory consubstantiality; the confusion between describer and described is essential to the work. Rousseau *must* be the person whose life and nature he presents, and if we do not believe it we are condemned to death forthwith. The basic assumption of his writing, moreover, is that the writer can in fact make the reader see Jean-Jacques directly, as if the reader himself were Jean-Jacques. In the *Dialogues,* however, a significant change takes place. The author recognizes and dramatizes the existence of *two* separate components of his identity: an isolated, subjective self, and a social self possessing a set of conventions (language, structured thought, modalities of relationship) that permit a mediation between the inner self and the outside world. In a sense, the duality implicit in the image of Rousseau standing before mankind with a self-portrait in his hand has evolved into an explicit recognition of a split in identity. The figure "Rousseau" of the *Dialogues,* like the author of the *Confessions,* points to "Jean-Jacques," whose existence for us consists of "Rousseau's" representation of him to the Frenchman; he is therefore as much an artifact as the book. To this extent, the preamble to the *Confessions* points towards the *Dialogues,* but in a veiled, symbolic manner. In the latter work, the illusion of consubstantiality of author and figure is destroyed, and "Rousseau" alone is in direct communication with the Frenchman. The social self (bearing, as is fitting, the family name), reflects upon the inner self and communicates this reflection to the outside world, acting as interpreter and agent. The inner self, "Jean-Jacques," is seen only by "Rousseau"; no one else may approach him directly. The outer self laboriously communicates to the outside world its knowledge of the inner self, and works in the service of the inner self (in the instance, to attain the writer's goal of being known, perhaps forgiven, certainly loved). It does so by pointing to the inner self and describing as best it can what it sees.

Rousseau is dramatizing here an inevitability of human existence, the split produced by reflection, perceived with such anguish and analyzed with such brilliance in the Second Discourse. But in the *Dialogues,* he is still far from accepting the consequences of this split —the necessity of mediation between inner self and other— as inevitable and irremediable. Instead he labors hard to spawn a fantasy of reintegration, in which finally the Frenchman is brought, like "Rousseau," into direct contact with "Jean-Jacques." "Rousseau" and the Frenchman are, in the final pages of the work, indistinguishable. "Rousseau" proposes a pact whereby he and the Frenchman will form with "Jean-Jacques" a "société sincère et sans fraude." "Jean-Jacques," trusting them, will open his heart and they will work to transmit the truth about "Jean-Jacques" to future generations. The Frenchman will see Jean-Jacques from time to time, with prudence and precaution. And the Frenchman offers, to this end, to share with "Rousseau" the risks of holding "Jean-Jacques's" papers in trust.

If language and logic were capable of effecting a perfect mediation between Self and Other, they would succeed in this masterpiece of dialectic. And so they do, but only *within* the work itself, in the closed-off world of Rousseau's dream. The significance of the work resides in the radical modification that occurs in the Frenchman's vision and attitude as he comes to see "Jean-Jacques" through "Rousseau's" eyes. But the Frenchman is not the actual reader of the *Dialogues;* the reader remains outside, elusive and free.

That the Frenchman is one more permutation of Rousseau's ideal reader can be seen in the way he came into being. In the prefatory "Du sujet et de la forme de cet écrit" Rousseau states:

> J'ai souvent dit que si l'on m'eut donné d'un autre homme les idées qu'on a données de moi à mes contemporains, je ne me serois pas conduit avec lui comme ils font avec moi. Cette assertion a laissé tout le monde fort indifférent sur ce point, et je n'ai vu chez personne la moindre curiosité de savoir en quoi ma conduite eut différé de celle des autres, et quelles eussent été mes raisons. [26]

The Frenchman of the *Dialogues* behaves *as Rousseau would have behaved* towards someone in his own position; once again, Rousseau is talking to himself. In speaking of the interlocutor he has created, Rousseau remarks:

---

[26] Ibid., p. 661.

> J'ai même eu l'attention de le ramener à des sentiments
> plus raisonnables que je n'en ai trouvé dans aucun de
> ses compatriotes, et celui que j'ai mis en scène est tel
> qu'il seroit aussi heureux pour moi qu'honorable à son
> pays qu'il s'y en trouvât becaucoup qui l'imitassent. [27]

The Frenchman is Rousseau, and with a little luck many other
Frenchmen will become Rousseau as well. We see here a pro-
longation of Rousseau's desire to serve as model, to see those he
addresses incorporated into himself. The breakdown in the
distinction between Self and Other will insure perfect understanding. The only problem is that, as he admits at the beginning
of "Du sujet...," no one has in fact behaved towards him as
the Frenchman does. And it is doubtful, in spite of Rousseau's
fervent wish, that any reader of the *Dialogues* has ever chosen
to follow the Frenchman's example of radical conversion.

❖   ❖   ❖

Rousseau's sense of relationship with his real reader during
this period is not difficult to pick up if we analyze his statements
about the *Dialogues* in "Du sujet ..." and in the "Histoire du
précédent écrit." It is worth noting, to begin with, that the *Dialogues,* the "maddest" of Rousseau's works, solipsistic, sealed off from
reality, a complex fantasy of guilt, punishment, and forgiveness,
is nonetheless carefully framed inside a preface and a postscript
in which the awareness of the actual *reader* of the *Dialogues* is
paramount. Thus, the *Dialogues* represent a moment of crisis
in which the decisive confrontation between the ideal reader and
the real reader, foreshadowed in the *Emile,* finally takes place in
Rousseau's mind. Small wonder that the composition and eventual
destination of the *Dialogues* should have been, for Rousseau, the
occasion for such anguish. He is at long last raising questions
about his most cherished conviction, that the dream world is self-
sufficient and totally satisfactory. (Qualms about the solidity of
this conviction appear earlier in such oblique ways as his choosing
to end his novel with Julie's death and the dissolution of the

---

[27] Ibid., p. 663.

dream. But at no time had he faced his qualms in an area that touched him directly — perhaps as directly as any: his identity as a writer.)

The votive passage that Rousseau appended to "Du sujet et de la forme de cet écrit" conveys the situation of the writer in all its peculiarity:

> Si j'osois faire quelque prière à ceux entre les mains de qui tombera cet écrit, ce seroit de vouloir bien le lire tout entier avant que d'en disposer et même avant que d'en parler à personne; mais très sûr d'avance que cette grâce ne me sera pas accordée, je me tais, et remets tout à la providence. [28]

There are several elements in this brief passage that will recur as *Leitmotive* in the presentation of the *Dialogues*. A consideration of these elements will provide a clearer understanding of Rousseau's sense of his relationship to his reader in 1772-1776.

It is taken as axiomatic in this passage that the work is going to fall into someone's hands. Since this is a persistent obsession with Rousseau (from 1761 on), it must have considerable significance, beyond the common, question-begging observation that it reflects the author's paranoia. I would submit that the obsession with the theft of his writings, with the surreptitious and unauthorized reading of his writings, and with the inevitability of their "falling into someone's hands" covers devastating feelings of doubt and fear about *not* having a reader. These feelings can be accounted for in two ways. On the one hand, they are based on an unconscious recognition of the solipsistic nature of his rhetorical situation. Aware that he is dealing with an ideal reader, an extension of himself, Rousseau apprehends being snubbed in return by the real reader to whom he has neglected to address himself. The dream of the reader's ravishment of his work gives him the consoling assurance that, in spite of his exclusion of the reader, he will be read. On the other hand, the feelings betray a realistic uncertainty about finding a reader. But since the last thing in the world that Rousseau could tolerate was uncertainty,

---

[28] Ibid., p. 659.

he forges an obsessive conviction that his work *will* be read, no matter how hard he may try to prevent it.

The hidden desire for communication through his writings appears clearly in Rousseau's frenzied attempts to place them (the *Dialogues* in particular) in various hands. If he cannot establish contact with the outside world through his works, they become "useless." The question of the "use" to which he (or another) may put his *Dialogues* preoccupies him deeply in both preface and postcript:

> Que deviendra cet écrit? Quel usage en pourrai-je faire? Je l'ignore, et cette incertitude a beacoup augmenté le découragement qui ne m'a point quitté en y travaillant.

> Qui que vous soyez que le Ciel a fait l'arbitre de cet écrit, quelque usage que vous ayez résolu d'en faire [...]

> comment en pouvoir faire usage [...]

> je trouvai que c'étoit un grand avantage que mon manuscrit me fut resté pour en dispenser plus sagement, et voici l'usage que je résolus d'en faire.

> Je suis dispensé desormais de vains efforts pour leur faire connoitre la vérité qu'ils sont déterminés à rejetter toujours, mais je ne le suis pas de leur laisser les moyens d'y revenir autant qu'il dépend de moi, et c'est le dernier usage qui me reste à faire de cet écrit. [29]

Seen from a slightly different angle, this obsession with the *use* to be made of his work can be considered a last frantic effort to turn the hostile, silent, misunderstanding Other into the loving, approving, comprehending Self. Deep in Rousseau's mind there still resides the conviction that this piece of writing can eventually show men the truth, i. e., make men see him through his own eyes. Yet his concern with the use others will make of his work stems at least in part from a clear recognition that, realistically, there is nothing the author can do, once his work is published, to enforce the precise understanding of it that he

---

[29] Ibid., pp. 666, 974, 977, 981, 987.

wishes the reader to have. The reader must confront the work on his own, and this readerly autonomy, with its possibilities for misunderstanding and rejection, must have terrified Rousseau.

The votive paragraph quoted earlier gives an indication of the conflict within Rousseau at this time. Wanting on the one hand still to control the reader, to insure a "proper" reading, he is already sure of failure: "mais très sûr d'avance que cette grâce ne me sera pas accordée, je me tais, et remets tout à la providence." If he were in fact "très sûr," he would not bother to express the wish. Both the preface and the postscript are filled with similar curious contradictions expressing at the same time a hope and a relinquishment of hope.

In his final reliance on providence, Rousseau is of course holding on to the fantasy of perfect communication. God, the ideal reader, understands and loves, and, being good, He will so guide events that one day men, whose minds are now veiled, will understand Rousseau just as He does. Yet it is most reveal-ing that Rousseau, in deciding to place his manuscript in the hands of providence by laying it on the high altar of Notre-Dame de Paris, also has in mind, and very clearly in mind, the pos-sibility that by so doing he may acquire as his reader the king himself. The king would be a *real* reader (albeit a most unlikely one) and Rousseau might be able to expect a practical response from him. Did the king not have the power to right wrongs?

When Rousseau finds his way to the high altar blocked by a grating, he undergoes a sudden crisis of relationship, minutely described in the "Histoire du précédent écrit." However one may interpret this crisis, and whatever degree of importance one may accord it, it surely marks a turning point in his relationship with the reader. In his pursuit of the captivating fantasy of union and transparency, Rousseau has reached the confines of the ima-ginable — presenting his work to God. The only way left is the way back. Concomitantly, he has pushed the conflict between ideal and real reader (in the instance, God and king) to the point where one of the opposing vectors in the conflict must cede to the other. The crisis in rhetorical orientation that surfaces in the *Emile* is at last to be resolved.

Rousseau's path back to communication with the real, auto-nomous reader takes at first the naive, dramatic, but understandable form of an attempt to actually *hand* his writings to another human being. He gives a copy of his *Dialogues* first to Condillac and then to Boothby, a young Englishman passing through Paris. In each case he considers his attempt unsuccessful: Condillac doesn't understand the work ("Il me parla de cet écrit comme il m'auroit parlé d'un ouvrage de littérature [...] il ne me dit rien de l'effet qu'avoit fait sur lui mon écrit, ni de ce qu'il pensoit de l'auteur"); [30] Boothby falls victim to Rousseau's persistent suspicion, and cannot be the proper recipient of the *Dialogues*. Next, he conceives and carries out that strange project of handing out in the street a "billet circulaire" addressed to "every Frenchman who still loves justice and truth." In content, the letter is a brief, emotional statement of Rousseau's situation (as he sees it), an accusation of cruelty, and a plea for compassion and understanding. It would be hard to find another spectacle that combines in such nice proportions the pathetic, the comical, and the courageous. Rousseau himself, as he relates it, was forced to laugh in the midst of his grief when nearly all the strangers he accosted, seeing the stated qualification of the addressee ("aimant encore la justice et la vérité"), declared themselves disqualified. Still, Rousseau continues in his attempt to transmit the letter, sending it to strangers who write him or who come to visit him. In each case, he is dissatisfied with the response.

It is not, however, Rousseau's satisfaction or dissatisfaction with the response to his circular letter that is important here, but rather the sudden, dogged attempt on his part to communicate directly with living creatures of his own species. It is significant that while in the *Dialogues* he addressed himself to "le Français," who is clearly a fiction, one of those creatures of his "monde des chimères," he should address himself in the circular letter to a definable group of actual Frenchmen. If he fails in his attempts to communicate with them, it is only because (as with Condillac, whom he unfairly put in the position of having to guess that the *Dialogues* were not a work of literature but a gesture) they refuse to be blackmailed into meeting his terms. Of course the strangers on the street refused to fall into the obvious trap of declaring themselves morally special. Of course the casual corres-

---

[30] Ibid., p. 982.

pondents refused to buy Rousseau's good graces by giving a categorical answer to his letter (such was the price he exacted). In so doing, they were asserting their own autonomy. Rousseau's reaction to this last failure, however, is indicative of the change that has taken place in him:

> Ce dernier mauvais sucçés, qui devoit mettre le comble à mon desespoir, ne m'affecta point comme les précédens. En m'apprenant que mon sort étoit sans ressources il m'apprit à ne plus lutter contre la nécessité. Un passage de l'*Emile* que je me rappelai me fit rentrer en moi-même et m'y fit trouver ce que j'avois cherché vainement au dehors. Quel mal t'a fait ce complot? Que t'a-t-il ôté de toi? Quel membre t'a-t-il mutilé? Quel crime t'a-t-il fait commettre? Tant que les hommes n'arracheront pas de ma poitrine le cœur qu'elle enferme pour y substituer, moi vivant, celui d'un malhonnête homme, en quoi pourront-ils altérer, changer, detériorer mon être? Ils auront beau faire un J.J. à leur mode, Rousseau restera toujours le même en dépit d'eux.
>
> N'ai-je donc connu la vanité de l'opinion que pour me remettre sous son joug aux dépends de la paix de mon ame et du repos de mon cœur? Si les hommes veulent me voir autre que je ne suis, que m'importe? L'essence de mon être est-elle dans leurs regards? S'ils abusent et trompent sur mon compte les générations suivantes, que m'importe encore? Je n'y serai plus pour être victime de leur erreur. [31]

The "fate" to which Rousseau refers is the inability to make others see him as he wished to be seen. This is, in fact, man's fate, and Rousseau's major blind spot as a thinker and as a man is his incapacity to recognize the universal nature of his situation. But his recognition and final acceptance of opacity and of autonomy as an inevitable condition (a "nécessité) at least of his *own* existence makes possible a renunciation of his dream of appropriating the reader, of turning the reader into another self. It is instructive in this regard that he should speak here of "returning into himself" (the phrase he always used to describe the reintegration of the alienated individual), and that he learns

---

[31] Ibid., p. 985.

this lesson *from himself* (i. e., from a passage in the *Emile*). The recognition of his own autonomy, of his own freedom from appropriation by the Other, so movingly expressed in the realization that the essence of his being does not reside in "their" gaze, carries with it an implicit acceptance of the autonomy of the Other. Curiously enough, Rousseau has finally learned the lesson he had tried for years to teach mankind.

❖   ❖   ❖

The "Histoire du précédent écrit" serves as a transition from the *Dialogues* to the *Rêveries du promeneur solitaire,* and if the relationship of writer to reader in the latter work is radically different from the relationship we find in the preceding works, it is precisely because of Rousseau's renunciation, in the spring and early summer of 1776, of his dream of an ideal relationship with the ideal reader. Near the end of the "Histoire du précédent écrit" Rousseau observes, speaking of his remaining duties towards men: "Je suis dispensé desormais de vains efforts pour leur faire connoitre la vérité qu'ils sont déterminés à rejetter toujours [...]." [32] The dispensation to which he refers resembles somewhat Quixote's awakening from his obsessive delusion. Rousseau, like the Don, is as absolute in his rejection of the delusion as he was in its pursuit. But the renunciation of the dream and acceptance of reality provide both of them with peace of mind and the possibility of a happy death: "Que les hommes fassent desormais tout ce qu'ils voudront, après avoir fait moi ce que j'ai du, ils auront beau tourmenter ma vie, ils ne m'empêcheront pas de mourir en paix." [33]

---

[32] Ibid., p. 987.
[33] Ibid., p. 989.

CHAPTER IV

THE RESOLUTION

In approaching the *Rêveries du promeneur solitaire,* we must distinguish between Rousseau's own conscious notion of his relationship with his reader and the functional relationship that exists. Rousseau's own notion is unequivocally solipsistic: whereas Montaigne wrote for others, he is writing his rêveries for himself alone; through the reading of his rêveries, he will recapture the pleasure felt in writing them, and he will live with himself in another age as with a younger friend; he is tranquil now in the depths of the abyss, impassive as God himself; everything outside of himself is henceforth foreign to him.

A similar conception appears in Rousseau's sense of his relationship with his own writing. In the Deuxième Promenade he establishes an identity between self and book. The book is supposed to be a mere register of his own inner life. This awareness of being able to capture his own inner life provides him with a sanctuary of sorts. He retreats at last into the enchanted garden, the only "real" Clarens, the imaginary land after his heart. Rousseau recognizes, in essence, a profound truth: we have a single inviolable preserve, our own inner world whose gate we may close to anyone. Awareness becomes aware of its own autonomy, and Rousseau at last belongs to himself. In this sense, the *Rêveries* are a celebration of identity and of autonomy. There is, moreover, a significant difference between this work and preceding works in which Rousseau was also attempting to create an enchanted garden: here Rousseau recognizes that he is inevitably *alone* in this garden, that the creature according to his heart is in fact himself. Instead of attempting to reshape the outside world according to the demands of his fantasy, Rousseau accepts now the hard, irrefutable existence of the outside world and voluntarily goes to dwell in the "abyss." There is no pretense of omnipotence. Thus, he is reduced to talking to himself. "E se non ho chi m'oda, parlo d'amor con me," as Cherubino puts it.

The celebration of autonomy and of the relationship of self to self is, however, only one aspect of the *Rêveries*. Rousseau is, in fact, not nearly so isolated from the world or from his reader as he chooses to think and as he would have us think. In spite of his insistence that men no longer exist for him, nor he for them, in spite of his conviction of having abandoned the struggle to be seen and judged by others, and in spite of his stated intention of exploring only his own identity ("Mais moi, detaché d'eux et de tout, que suis-je en moi-même? Voilà ce qui me reste à chercher."),[1] Rousseau ceaselessly contemplates in his final work his relationship to that which is outside of him, be it man or nature. From Promenade to Promenade, he examines his relationship to his public, to animals, to vegetables, to minerals, to the Lake of Bienne, to a little boy on crutches, to his childhood playmates, to Mme de Warens; he works out, with a profundity that surpasses anything he had previously been capable of, the familiar questions of power relationships, the ethics of verbal communication, and the relation between self and external reality. Nowhere in his earlier works is he so candidly and profitably aware of relationship.

We may expect to find in the rhetorical situation of the work the same contradiction between stated isolation and functional relationship. The opening sentence itself sounds just this note of contradiction: "Me voici donc seul sur la terre" asserts solitude and implies relationship. Rousseau's gesture of pointing to himself (a frequent occurrence in the *Rêveries*) has significance only in terms of the presence of an outside observer. Similarly, the use of the definite article in the title (he is *the* solitary stroller) implies an identification of the author by contrast with another group from which he is distinguished and to which he is re-

---

[1] *O. C.* I, p. 995.

cognizable as "that person who takes walks all alone." A recurrent theme of the *Rêveries* will be, in fact, the constant attention and recognition given to the author on his strolls. Moreover, the description of his state that emerges from the work by no means justifies the negative attributes through which Rousseau consciously identifies himself ("n'ayant plus de frere, de prochain, d'ami, de société que moi-même"). Figures referred to in the various Promenades look suspiciously like a wife, fellowmen, and "société."

What are we to make of this discrepancy between the author's image of himself and the apparent reality of his state? The answer to this question lies, I believe, in the interpretation of the word *donc* figuring in the opening sentence. *Donc* implies a concatenation, seemingly out of place in an utterance without antecedent. We must then look for an antecedent outside of and, we may presume, immediately preceding the Première Promenade. The antecedent would thus appear to be the ending of the "Histoire du précédent écrit," written in June or July of 1776 and Rousseau's last writing prior to the *Rêveries*. The "Histoire du précédent écrit" ends, as we have seen, with Rousseau's relinquishment of the dream of transparency and with a concomitant declaration of autonomy. These decisions would inevitably given rise to a deep *sense* of solitude (felt positively as peace and negatively as loss, the two feelings that will alternate with each other throughout the *Rêveries*), however mitigated Rousseau's actual isolation may have been. In comparison with his dream of total communication and of assimilation of Other to Self, the slightest degree of separation and autonomy must have at least *felt* like total isolation. The post-Clarentian world seems cold and lonely: we should not forget that after the death of Julie, who had acted magically as the guarantor of transparency among the members of her little group, there appear strong hints of dissolution and isolation, and the novel ends with a haunting call to the grave. It is this *feeling* of desolation that Rousseau, in his usual subjectivist confusion, takes to be an accurate assessment of his situation. But although the feeling may be one of total solitude, the reality consists of a new kind of relationship, perceptible both in the biographical facts of the final two years of Rousseau's life (after twenty years of destroying old friendships he at last begins to form some new ones), in the preoccupations of the work (mentioned above), and in the rhetorical situation itself.

The word *donc* links the realization of solitude with a new enterprise made possible by this realization. According to Rousseau, the aim of his work is self-definition. But had not self-definition been Rousseau's central preoccupation from the *Lettres à Malesherbes* through the *Dialogues?* Unquestionably it had been to a large degree. But the effort at self-definition had been hobbled all along both by the element of self-justification and, still more seriously, by the effort to *abolish* the very distinction between Self and Other on which self-definition is predicated. [2] Having accepted this distinction as inevitable, Rousseau acquires the means for arriving at a considerably deeper and clearer assessment of his own identity. The *Rêveries* are, in his words, "la suite de l'examen sévére et sincére que j'appelai jadis mes *Confessions*"; [3] but by the time he composes the Quatrième Promenade he has recognized that the Know Thyself inscribed on the Temple at Delphi is not so easy a maxim to follow as he had thought in writing his *Confessions*. Indeed, the process of self-definition becomes difficult precisely when one recognizes the complex dynamics of relationship between Self and Other that serve as a basis for identity.

❋   ❋   ❋

Now, having abandoned his attempt to appropriate the reader, Rousseau is able to establish with him a simpler, more direct kind of relationship. The persuasive rhetoric of the early works, the Orphic stance of the *Emile*, the obsessive self-justification of the *Confessions* and the *Dialogues* are for the most part absent,

---

2 Rousseau recognized when he wrote the preamble to the Neuchâtel manuscript of the *Confessions* in 1764 that self-definition is possible only through comparison with non-self. In fact, his justification for describing himself is presented in terms of the useful point of comparison he will provide other men for their own attempt at self-definition. But, still caught up in his obsession with abolishing the distinction between Self and Other, he omits this notation from the final version of the preamble.

3 *O. C.* I, p. 999.

and the author communicates with a limpidity, a lyrical immediacy virtually without prior example in literature.

To be sure, there are residual traces of the earlier rhetorical elements. Rousseau still feels some need to combat his enemies' deformations by placing the *truth* before the reader. In the Deuxième Promenade, for example, he gives a minute account of the accident during the summer of 1776 in which he was knocked down by a dog, and ends with the notation: "Voilà très fidèlement le recit de mon accident." [4] Although not addressing the reader directly, he is nonetheless presenting his account for someone's enlightenment, as if to set things straight. In this instance, there was good reason for providing his own "authorized" version, since (as he goes on to note) all kinds of rumors, including the gleeful news of his death, began to circulate as soon as the accident was known. Even here, however, the writer is merely placing the material at the reader's disposal. There is no insistence or even implication that the reader *must* believe Rousseau's version under pain of being considered an "homme à étouffer." Editors of the *Rêveries* tend to comment smilingly on Rousseau's evident concern with self-justification in a work that opens with a proclamation of unconcern about other men and their opinions. [5] Admittedly, Rousseau is fair game on this point. But we should not, in our eagerness to catch the old rascal in an inconsistency, overlook the fundamental change in his manner of presenting self-justificatory material. Where before he had attempted to force the reader to accept the writer's truth, he is now willing merely to leave the reader a register of the writer's own vision of himself.

✿ ✿ ✿

---

[4] Ibid., p. 1006.

[5] Jean Guéhenno, for example, would have it that Rousesau suffered, after so much glory, from the silence and obscurity of his final years (*Rêveries du promeneur solitaire*, Paris, Editions de la Bibliothèque Mondiale, 1956, unpaginated introduction). We should, I think, be careful of Grimm's malicious account, accepted by M. Guéhenno without question, of Rousseau's supposed obscurity and of his supposed reaction to it as a blow to his vanity. Grimm had hated Rousseau for years, and now, fearing the publication of the *Confessions*, must have been sharpening his axe to a fine edge indeed. (For Grimm's comment, see the *Correspondance Littéraire*, June, 1776 [vol. XI, pp. 283-289 in the Garnier edition of 1879]).

In the *Rêveries,* direct evidence of Rousseau's awareness of his reader (as, for example, apostrophe, so common in the earlier works) is not to be found. Abundant evidence appears, however, in stylistic features of the work. The frequent use of maxim and aphorism points toward a figure outside the work, a figure standing in for the generality of mankind to which the universal statement applies. Maxims and aphorisms imply solidarity, since their validity stretches beyond the individual experience and use of the writer. When Rousseau states: "Le bonheur est un état permanent qui ne semble pas fait ici bas pour l'homme," [6] he is giving the lie to the assertion of complete isolation with which he begins his final work. He is involved in mankind, and although a shaman determined never to return to his tribesmen, he nonetheless thinks of, works for, and continues to send messages back to them.

Although the dominant personal mode of the *Rêveries* is the first-person singular (logically so since Rousseau is usually relating his own feelings and experiences), in a number of statements the *je* is replaced by generalizers such as *on, soi, l'homme,* or impersonal verb forms. When Rousseau exclaims: "Helas, c'est quand on commence à quitter sa dépouille qu'on en est le plus offusqué!" [7] he is by no means obliged to couch his observation in general terms. Indeed, considering the prevailingly personal mode, we would tend rather to expect the usual *je* ("C'est quand je quitte..."), and the solidarity of *on* is all the more striking.

Other locutions imply the existence of a reader. "Cette découverte n'étoit pas si facile à faire qu'on pourroit le croire [...]": [8] with whose opinion is Rousseau concerned here, if not with that of one who is "listening in"? Similarly, when he states: "Oui, je le dis et le sens avec une fière élevation d'ame [...]," [9] he is not throwing the affirmation into a void. Even the manner of setting forth material by way of a gesture ("Telles furent mes régles de conscience sur le mensonge et sur la vérité") [10] implies a presentation to someone.

---

[6] *O. C.* I, p. 1085.
[7] Ibid., p. 1049.
[8] Ibid., p. 1079.
[9] Ibid., p. 1035.
[10] Ibid., p. 1032.

Rousseau's assurances of his own complete veracity carry with them additional indication of a "presence" outside of the work. Speaking of his feelings and moral intent in the episode of his lie about the stolen ribbon, for example, he introduces his affirmation with an oath: "Je puis jurer à la face du ciel qu'à l'instant même où cette honte invincible me l'arrachoit j'aurois donné tout mon sang avec joye pour en détourner l'effet sur moi seul." [11] The oath implies a spectator or witness, such as one finds in the preamble to the *Confessions*. Examples of this sort abound in the *Rêveries*. The difference between this work and the *Confessions*, however, lies in the fact that here, although still holding on to the figure of the witness, Rousseau no longer appears to be challenging him to a moral duel. The writing of the *Rêveries* is not the occasion for an assertion of superiority over the reader. Nor is it the occasion for an exhibitionistic gesture aimed at eliciting a reciprocal uncovering, a comparison.

The anticipated objection, typical of the *Emile* and the *Confessions*, and an essential component of the *Dialogues* (which begin, in fact, with a tirade against Jean-Jacques), appears in the *Rêveries* as well, giving further evidence of Rousseau's awareness of a reader. Here, however, the objections generally represent legitimate, sensible questions that any man of good faith might pose. Rousseau does not appear to be anticipating that the reader will attempt to trap him in one contradiction or another, but merely that the reader will want to know how a contradiction is to be avoided: "Mais, diroit-on, comment accorder ce relâchement avec cet ardent amour pour la vérité dont je le glorifie? Cet amour est donc faux puisqu'il souffre tant d'alliage? Non, il est pur et vrai: mais il n'est qu'une émanation de l'amour de la justice et ne veut jamais être faux quoiqu'il soit souvent fabuleux." [12] Judging by the nature and tone of the interrogatives, and by the simplicity of the response, Rousseau is no longer dealing with a reader whose obtuseness and ill-will serve only to satisfy the writer's own fantasy of miscomprehension. And in this lower-keyed, friendlier relationship, Rousseau conceives of a reader more closely resembling a real human being than did either of the fantasy readers,

---

[11] Ibid., p. 1025.
[12] Ibid., pp. 1031-2.

the one completely isolated and hostile, the other wired for perfect communication. Rousseau now seems to conceive of a reader who needs explanations not through any peculiar fault of his own, but because of the inevitable condition of separateness. Furthermore, the very indeterminacy of the reader's identity (sharply contrasting with the obsessive precision with which Rousseau had formerly identified the sheep for whom he was writing and the goats for whom he was not writing) seems to indicate a new-found respect for the integrity of each individual reader. He makes it possible for the reader to approach the work without abjuring his own identity.

Precisely because of this freedom granted the reader, it is difficult to assign him specific features. No longer the spurious "convinceable" reader of the *Emile,* nor his opaque and obtuse counterpart, nor the Frenchman of the *Dialogues* whose conversion from enemy to friend comforts Rousseau, the reader of the *Rêveries* is faceless, or as if hidden behind a screen. He seems to be present as an eavesdropper who may make what he will of what he hears. But the writer knows that he is being listened to. Out of the corner of his eye, he watches the "on" and the "ils" to whom he refers throughout the work. The *Rêveries* are to some extent then written *for* Rousseau's tormentors: the writer is still motivated by a desire to assert his autonomy in the face of a hostile world (in direct continuation of the attitude expressed at the close of the "Histoire du précédent écrit"). Rousseau's supposed "indifference" to the world around him is somewhat too loudly proclaimed to be convincing. The truth of the matter is that the *Rêveries* betray an element of defiance and revenge. In the Septième Promenade, speaking of his renewed interest in botany, Rousseau observes: "Je ne cherche pas à justifier le parti que je prends de suivre cette fantaisie [...] C'est me venger de mes persecuteurs à ma manière, et je ne saurois les punir plus cruellement que d'être heureux malgré eux." [13] The vengeance has little significance except in so far as Rousseau's tranquillity "in spite of them" is observed. The spuriousness of his "indifference" emerges as well from a passage in the Huitième Promenade:

---

[13] Ibid., p. 1061.

Comment vivre heureux et tranquille dans cet état affreux [i. e., the state to which his enemies have reduced him]? J'y suis pourtant encore et plus enfoncé que jamais, et j'y ai retrouvé le calme et la paix et j'y vis heureux et tranquille et j'y ris des incroyables tourmens que mes persecuteurs se donnent sans cesse tandis que je reste en paix, occupé de fleurs, d'etamines et d'enfantillages et que je ne songe pas même à eux. [14]

The final proposition ("je ne songe pas même à eux") is untenable, for Rousseau is obviously thinking of his persecutors throughout the *Rêveries,* if only to state, as here, his indifference to them.

In a sense, the *Rêveries* constitute a reenactment of the *Dialogues.* Both works embody a quadruple relationship. In the earlier work the Frenchman and "Rousseau" are placed directly before the reader, while "Jean-Jacques" and the Public are known only as off-stage antagonists. In the *Rêveries,* the Frenchman has been replaced by the hidden *persona* of the reader whose existence is disclosed through the style, and the Public has been reduced to the nameless, faceless "on" and "ils." More precisely still, the polar figures of the ultimately sympathetic Frenchman (who enters into communication with Jean-Jacques) and the absolutely hostile Public (which remains sealed off from Jean-Jacques) move towards each other to engender on the one hand the unseen but unbiased reader and on the other the observing crowd, still "hostile" but now close enough to witness the gesture of defiance. Both components of the self are present as well in the later work, no longer dramatized, however, as separate figures. One is the reflecting, describing agent, the other is the subject of the reflection and description. The writer (agent and interpreter) points to the subject (the topic of the work) for his own and the reader's benefit, defining the subject in terms of his attributes and in terms of his relationship, lack of relationship, or limited relationship with "on." The work is thus a continuous gesture by which the writer directs our gaze towards his own identity. To this extent the similarity with the *Dialogues* is evident.

The crucial difference between the *Dialogues* and the *Rêveries* lies in the reestablishment of contact in the later work between

---

[14] Ibid., p. 1076.

two "selves" of Rousseau and between the writer and reader.
The reintegration of Rousseau's identity is signified in the "Histoire
du précédent écrit" by the use of both first and last name to
designate *one and the same person:* "Ils auront beau faire un
J.J. à leur mode, Rousseau restera toujours le même en dépit
d'eux." [15] As far as I have been able to make out, in his final
work Rousseau designates himself by either first or last name at
random. Both now equal *moi:* the inner and outer self are no
longer felt as separate people. Still, they have separate functions
within the same personality. In terms of the rhetorical situation,
the social identity is the writer-self (which was, after all, Rousseau's most genuine and effective social role) and the matter of
the book is the subject-self. There is, to be sure, a time lapse
between the actual stroll during which Rousseau has delved into
himself ("returned into himself," as he always conceived it) and
the setting down of his musings in an organized, comprehensible
form. This distinction is unavoidable, and it underscores the
fundamental difference between the state of "being lost in
thought" and the action of communicating that state to others
(in the instance, to the reader). A passage from the Fourth Book
of the *Confessions* illustrates, by way of contrast with what we
see in the *Rêveries,* the difference between pure fantasy and later
externalization of fantasy:

> La chose que je regrette le plus dans les détails de
> ma vie dont j'ai perdu la mémoire est de n'avoir pas fait
> des journaux de mes voyages. Jamais je n'ai tant pensé,
> tant existé, tant vécu, tant été moi, si j'ose ainsi dire,
> que dnas ceux que j'ai faits seul et à pied. La marche
> a quelque chose qui anime et avive mes idées; je ne puis
> presque penser quand je reste en place; il faut que mon
> corps soit en branle pour y mettre mon esprit [...]. Je
> dispose en maitre de la nature entière; mon coeur errant
> d'objet en objet s'unit, s'identifie à ceux qui le flatent,
> s'entoure d'images charmantes, s'enivre de sentimens
> délicieux. Si pour les fixer je m'amuse à les décrire en
> moi-même, quelle vigueur de coloris, quelle énergie d'ex-
> pression je leur donne! On a, dit-on, trouvé de tout cela
> dans mes ouvrages quoiqu'écris vers le declin de mes ans.

---

[15] Ibid., p. 985.

O si l'on eut vû ceux de ma prémière jeunesse, ceux que
j'ai faits durant mes voyages, ceux que j'ai composés et
que je n'ai jamais écrits... pourquoi, direz-vous, ne
les pas écrire? et pourquoi les écrire, vous répondrai-je:
Pourquoi m'ôter le charme actuel de la jouissance pour
dire à d'autres que j'avois joui? Que m'importaient des
lecteurs, un public et toute la terre, tandis que je plânois
dans le Ciel? D'ailleurs portois-je avec moi du papier,
des plumes? Si j'avois pensé à tout cela rien ne me seroit
venu. [16]

The inspirational virtue of strolling has remained the same for
Rousseau. The new element is his willingness to set down the
results of his inspiration for another to share. Analyzing the terms
of his argument, we see that the Rousseau of 1766 was disinclined
to forego some of the immediate enjoyment of his daydreams
and to contaminate the pure pleasure with the effort of recollec-
tion and externalization. The very intention to communicate, to
share, would inevitably have brought with it a preoccupation,
from the start, with form, an auto-critical process typical of
artistic creation but not of free fantasy. Rousseau is not yet ready
to give up the exalting sense of omnipotence that flowed from the
experience of unimpeded daydreaming. He still wishes, in 1766,
to "disposer en maître de la nature entière." But it is significant
that already he anticipates a reproach from his reader: "Pourquoi, direz-vous, ne les pas écrire?" Is he perhaps failing in his
responsibility as an author? Ten years later, his readers have
apparently become sufficiently important to him to bring about
a revision of the principle guiding his work, and he has exchanged
the earlier inebriation, the sense of total domination and identification, for the less heady but also less ephemeral, less solitary
satisfaction of recreating his daydream for another. In the earlier
passage, the author's reminiscence of his charming mental strolls
of his youth begins, significantly, with an expression of *regret*
at not having set them down in a journal. Thus, in his final work,
the "journal informe de [ses] rêveries," he acts upon his regret,
and sets things right by giving his fellowmen the precious gift,

---

[16] Ibid., p. 162.

not of a doctrine, not of an apology, but of himself, his thoughts and feelings.

The effort involved in the process of reduplication in organized form can be seen in the careful revisions Rousseau made of his *Rêveries,* in certain instances choosing and discarding several times before arriving at the definitive reading. In this regard, the revision of the opening paragraph of the Sixième Promenade is revealing. Originally, the Promenade began with the second sentence of the definitive version: "Hier passant sur le nouveau boulevard pour aller herboriser le long de la Bievre de Gentilli, je fis le crochet à droite en approchant de la barrière d'enfer, et m'écartant dans la campagne j'allai par la route de Fontainebleau gagner les hauteurs qui bordent cette petite rivière." [17] In the final version, there is an introductory sentence: "Nous n'avons guére de mouvement machinal dont nous ne pussions trouver la cause dans notre cœur, si nous savions bien l'y chercher." The writer has sacrificed the mere reduplication of his experience, in which the pen moving across the paper does no more than happily reenact the movement of his stroll, in order to prepare his reader for the main point of the opening section (which Rousseau himself, of course, already knows). The process of "artifaction" is motivated by a desire to shape the writer's experience for the reader.

The *Rêveries* demonstrate throughout a high awareness of composition. Rousseau is structuring his object with the purpose of having it perceived *thus* and not otherwise. Implicit in this shaping is a recognition of the fact that the "self" which we present to the world is to some extent an artifact. We are forced to fix that which is fluid and elusive; we are forced to conventionalize by use of language (our principle tool for the externalization and even the exploration of the self) that which is not by nature conventional; we contaminate, if only to the slightest degree, our representation through shame, fear, etc. The process of self-description found in the *Rêveries* is no exception to the rule. Rousseau's triumph, however, lies in his final acceptance of this inevitable fact of life. His acceptance may not be fully conscious,

---

[17] Ibid., p. 1050.

but an analysis of his artistic operations tells us all we need to know of it. At last he assumes, as a writer, that communication is at best relative and imperfect. One can do no more than describe oneself with all available courage and accuracy, and hope that others will see more or less what has been described. Rousseau has resigned himself, in the *Rêveries*, to being seen otherwise than as he is ("ils ne verront jamais à ma place que le J.J. qu'ils se sont fait et qu'ils ont fait selon leur cœur, pour le haïr à leur aise"). [18] As usual, he sees the situation in absolute terms: unable to see him as he sees himself, "they" must necessarily see him as someone totally different. But precisely the acceptance of this absurd and perpetual quiproquo allows him to describe himself more freely than before, and by and large without the anguish that grew out of his frustrated aspiration to be known *sub specie Dei*.

* * *

In the *Rêveries*, then, the reader appears neither as enemy nor as friend, but as spectator, with all the limitations inherent in the role. He is a witness primarily not to Rousseau's goodness or innocence, but to Rousseau's *being*, as this being knows and represents itself. And if a certain amount of self-justification still enters into the depiction, it is now because of Rousseau's own need to believe in his goodness and innocence. He still must be the "man of nature and truth" if his own life and his notion of the world is to make any sense at all to him. No longer does it appear so important, however, to make others recognize these attributes. If Rembrandt endowed his face, in his later self-portraits, with an ineffably sad serenity, it was surely not to convince another of his sad serenity, but to give a faithful representation of his own vision of himself. So with Rousseau. The fundamental motive is that of self-recognition and self-definition. [19]

---

18 Ibid., p. 1059.

19 In speaking of his renewed interest in botanizing, he remarks: "c'est une bizarrerie que je voudrois m'expliquer; il me semble que, bien eclaircie, elle pourroit jetter quelque nouveau jour sur cette connoissance de moi-même à l'acquisition de laquelle j'ai consacré mes derniers loisirs (ibid., p. 1061). Self-knowledge is given precisely as the reason for the rêverie.

The externalization of the recognition serves to introduce Self to Other. And a self-portrait of this kind simply proclaims its own existence, without calling for any pre-determined response.

I stated earlier that the *Confessions* also provided the reader with a faithful portrait of the author. What, then, distinguishes them from the *Rêveries?* What does the later work add to the earlier? It adds precisely nothing. In it, Rousseau removes those elements which, although intended to insure proper vision on the reader's part, constitute an obstacle, an interference of sorts in the process of communication. Just as the chronological gap between the writer and the matter is narrower in the *Rêveries* than in the *Confessions* (in that the former is an account of the current daydream, and the latter an account of past events), so is the difference between work and reader. To pursue the analogy with the visual portrait, it is as if in one version the artist surrounded his image with a wealth of iconography (a halo, a book of law, etc.) intended to direct the viewer's attention to precisely those qualities that he is to see in the figure, whereas in a later version the artist leaves only the figure for the viewer to perceive. If, as stated earlier, Rousseau had been forced in his *Confessions* to turn himself into an object, *his* object, in order to avoid being seen as his enemies' object, in the *Rêveries* he again becomes an object but this time not through a movement of self-defense. Instead it is through a dual movement of self-recognition and self-presentation, the one barely distinguishable from the other. And this time the object does not possess the peculiarly static quality of the object in the *Confessions* (where even the contradictory qualities of the memorialist exist as if in a permanently moulded figure). One derives from a reading of the *Rêveries* a sense of the fluidity, the three-dimensionality of a figure that knows itself in the flow of time and the mystery of human depth. A premise of the self-definition in the *Rêveries* is that the self ultimately escapes perfect definition, that the means of description are imperfect and the process never-ending. The Rousseau of the *Confessions* fled from ambiguity. The Rousseau of the *Rêveries* incorporates it into his vision of himself. He is willing at last to see himself, and to present himself to the

reader, not as a statue but as the creature of unsounded depths
that he knows himself to be.

*   *   *

No study of Rousseau can claim to be final. The sense of a
major author's writings, from whatever point of view they may
be approached, defies positive codification. I have attempted in
this study, which is a meditation on the *transmission* of Rousseau's
own meditations, merely to suggest a useful and valid way of
looking at the subject. And I hope in the process to have broken
ground for further investigation, whether it be in the nature of
clarification, development, or revision. Already there occur to me
various possibilities for further study. The first would be a
systematic and comprehensive stylistic analysis of individual works
and, eventually, of the whole corpus of works with the aim of
ascertaining the relative importance of traditional rhetoric and
precepts of composition at various stages in Rousseau's writing.
In other words, how does the man who in his early twenties made
a conscious effort to model his style on that of Voltaire finish by
writing the *Confessions* and, especially, the *Rêveries?* What may
this evolution have to do with an intuitive recognition of the
inadequacy of the inherited modes of literary communication to
new modes of feeling and thought? Any consideration of Rousseau
from this point of view should do much to illuminate the larger
problems of language and style in the 18th Century. A second
object of study, which will be feasible once the computerized
vocabulary analysis of Rousseau's writings now in preparation is
finished, might be the frequency of lexical items in relation to the
rhetorical situation. Can we find, for example, significant lexical
distinctions (leaving aside, of course, heavy frequencies dictated
by the choice of subject) in terms of the reader whom Rousseau is
addressing? A third possibility for consideration: what variations
in the rhetorical situation are to be found within the body of
the correspondence? (Again, the reliable text of the *Correspondance complète* currently appearing will provide the basis for
such a study.) Finally, it would be most useful to have a specific
study of Rousseau's practice of communication through language
in the light of his own theoretical statements, as well as in the

light of the theoretical statements of such men as Condillac and Diderot, on the nature of language, its functioning, and its relationship to reality.

All of the problems mentioned bristle with difficulties and tantalize with perhaps unverifiable conjectures, but are nonetheless well worth investigation. Perhaps the present study will succeed in stimulating interest in them.